STUDIES IN ENGLISH AND AMERICAN
LITERATURE, LINGUISTICS, AND CULTURE

VOL. 2

STUDIES IN ENGLISH AND AMERICAN LITERATURE, LINGUISTICS, AND CULTURE

Vol. 2

Editorial Board

CAMDEN HOUSE
Columbia, South Carolina

Intruder into Eden

WOODCUT OF TITLE CHARACTER, IGNORAMUS (1630)
Printed with permission of William R. Perkins Library, Duke University

Intruder into Eden:

Representations of
The Common Lawyer in English Literature
1350-1750

E.F.J. Tucker

CAMDEN HOUSE

Set in Garamond type
and printed on acid-free paper.

In Memoriam

Jessie E.M. Tucker
Nelle M. Krise
Mary June Flynn

Contents

Abbreviations

AJLH American Journal for Legal History

CLJ Cambridge Law Journal

EETS Early English Text Society

o.s. Old Series

e.s. Extra Series

EHR English Historical Review

HEL Sir William Holdsworth. *The History of English Law*. 12 vols. London: Methuen, 1903-1938.

HLQ Huntington Library Quarterly

LQR Law Quarterly Review

PMLA Publications of the Modern Language Association

POAS Poems on Affairs of State ed. George deF. Lord, et al. 7 vols. New Haven: Yale University Press, 1963-1980.

SS Publications of the Selden Society

Preface

I HAVE EMPLOYED the term "representations" in the title as a way of reminding myself, with William of Occam, that *"essentia non sunt multiplicanda praeter necessitatem"* and that noun phrases, like "the common lawyer," while serving as useful labels, do not refer to any particular reality but like algebraic symbols represent a great diversity of meanings conventionally shared and recognized. Nor is the common lawyer the sole creation of literary artists and critics, for he is a composite representation, or a set of public images, historically determined by the reactions of men and women in all walks of life in response to the professional conduct of lawyers. He is the subject of jokes, common gossip, sermons, philosophical treatises, newspaper articles, art, and even of his own professional literature; and it is from the sheer abundance of these popular sources, each of which contributes to the composite representation, that authors have created their own portraits of literary lawyers. However, since the lawyer, from a very early period, becomes a conventional figure, with distinct characteristics, he tends to move independently within in his own literary sphere. This seems especially true of satirical portraiture which perpetuates the conventional representation long after it is historically and realistically accurate in terms of social and professional criticism. Thus, it is necessary to interpret the lawyer's literary role and characterization both from a literary and a social/historical perspective.

It was, I believe, the multifaceted character of the literary lawyer which prompted me to adopt a thematic rather than a chronological structure for the book as the design which would best enable me to examine each facet of the composite representation sequentially. Each chapter is also designed to trace the genealogy of a representation historically from the time of Chaucer to the age of Johnson. However, by analyzing each major representation in turn, including the pettifogger, the ignoramus, the diabolical lawyer, and the lawyer-lover, I do not wish to suggest that the classifications or types chosen are in any way distinct, for they may appear in any combination. Thus, the pettifogger may be diabolically inspired, or the ignoramus may prove to be relatively harmless or even honest.

In the history and development of any particular kind of satire, the critic is likely to find a remarkable consistency in his subject matter, and it is this consistency which threatens the historical study of satire with the possibility of monotonous repetition. The critic is automatically confronted with notorious difficulties of organization, particularly if he opts for a chronological approach. Works on political satire seem rather humdrum to the reader because graft is graft no matter how one divides and subdivides it. Even though opportunities for political corruption are inexhaustible, the satirical representations tend to remain relatively constant. Thus, critical treatments of satire, if they aspire to scholarly completeness, often deteriorate into mere lists of authors, titles, and plots bulked out with carefully chosen quotations. In this book, I have attempted to avoid these pitfalls by adopting a thematic structure.

After ten years of intensive reading and reflection, involving two grants from the National Endowment for the Humanities and a Dexter Grant from Harvard University, I had amassed such a volume of notes that I was forced to divide my work into two consecutive projects, the first of which is embraced in this monograph. In other words, I have chosen to culminate this portion of my studies during the age of Johnson for two reasons: first, because the original book was growing to unmanageable length, far beyond any reasonable expectation of publication; second, because the literary history of lawyers takes on a vastly new significance during the great age of legal reforms which began with the work of Bentham and Romilly and culminated in the sweeping changes of the Judicature Acts of 1873 and 1874. Therefore, I have reserved this portion of my work for a second book which will continue the story into the early twentieth century. The brief epilogue I supply here anticipates some of the major preoccupations of later writers.

I have also avoided a number of other dangerous temptations, the most serious of which is the Casaubon-like desire for scholarly completeness. On certain topics, the material proved so plentiful that it would have been supremely easy to proliferate quotations and footnotes to the point of suffocation. I also decided, quite deliberately, to exclude all the material I had gathered on the history of civil and canon lawyers, most of which in any case merely confirms those representational aspects here developed for the common lawyer. Finally, for the most part, I have resisted the obvious temptation of straying too deeply into the purely political dimensions of legal practice; and where I have devoted some space to such great political lawyers as Wolsey, More, Coke, Bacon, and Mansfield, I have tried to place the greater stress upon the legal issues involved.

I am deeply grateful for the expert and cordial assistance I have received at the numerous research libraries I have visited, including those at Harvard, Yale, Chicago, Duke, and the University of South Carolina in this country, and the

British Library, the Bodleian, and the Cambridge University Library in Great Britain. Herb Nath of the Daniel Library at the Citadel has given me invaluable assistance in supplying me with books and xeroxed articles during those extended periods when I have been unable to travel. I am also indebted to Southern Methodist University, East Tennessee State University, and The Citadel Development Foundation for the supplementary funds needed for travel and research, and also to Harvard University and the National Endowment for Humanities. I would also like to thank the editors of the *Harvard Library Bulletin, Renaissance Quarterly,* and *Modern Philology* (copyright by The University of Chicago Press, 1981) for their permission to use portions of articles published in their journals. For permission to print the woodcut of Ignoramus as my frontispiece, I am grateful to the curator and staff, particularly to Ms. Erin Echols, at the Rare Book Room of the William R. Perkins Library, Duke University.

Although it would be impossible to mention all the colleagues who have made a contribution, either in moral or substantive terms, towards the completion of this book, I would like to acknowledge indebtedness to Ambrose N. Manning of East Tennessee State, John M. Wallace of Chicago, Ian Jack and John H. Baker of Cambridge, and G. Blakemore Evans of Harvard, all of whom have read and offered useful comments on the text. I would also like to thank my editor, Benjamin Franklin of Camden House, for his expert and courteous guidance in bringing this study to what I hope is a satisfactory conclusion. Any errors and inconsistencies remaining in the text are entirely my own. I am also deeply grateful to John H. Baker, David Yale, and Michael Prichard for allowing me to participate in their legal history seminars at the University of Cambridge in 1974-1975. Finally, I am eternally in debt to my wife Cathy and my children Ellen and Ian for their steadfast, patient, and loving support through the many trying months of forced absence and isolation.

1

Satire and the Law: Grounds for Criticism
Law and the Golden Age

The Hidden Law does not deny
Our laws of probability,
But takes the atom and the star
And human beings as they are,
And answers nothing when we lie.

It is the only reason why
No government can codify
And legal definitions mar
The Hidden Law.
W. H. Auden, "The Hidden Law"

TO THE PRACTICING LAWYER, hardened by years of wrestling with real cases and
procedural minutiae, an accurate definition of the term *law* might seem the most
inconsequential of issues. Historically, the English lawyer has been content to
leave such lofty matters to the legal philosophers. If pressed, however, he might
insist that the law is a reasonably exact social science based upon the formulation
of rules as determined by precise standards of equality, certainty, and
universality, further modified by principles of equity. He may concede that errors
in judgment sometimes occur in terms of a popular view of justice, yet he would
emphatically insist that the legal machine is constantly reestablishing its
equilibrium, even though an odd injustice occasionally squirts out at the seams.

Inasmuch as lawyers are human, Auden is correct, for no science is correct, no lawyer or judge infallible. Indeed, there are times when the man of law may well command our sympathy for the severity of criticism directed against him. Like the churchman and the teacher, he is constantly abused and denigrated by "those in the know." Professional knowledge and experience are seldom appreciated by the ignorant and the profane, and many of the adverse criticisms leveled at the common lawyer can thus be summarily dismissed.

In "Law like Love," Auden attacks the post-Austinian doctrine of judicial certainty by reducing the authoritarian judge, after many false starts at a definition, to the lame conclusion that "law is the Law." Like love, justice or the "hidden law" is an ideal essence, indefinable, inescapable, and supernal.[1] For the ancient Greeks, the spirit of justice that informs the law, which they represented in the form of the virgin Astraea, had fled from the world's corruption at the end of the Golden Age, never to return. In Christian tradition, justice had been destroyed by original sin and resides only in the inscrutable mind of God. Christians were admonished to avoid lawsuits (1 Cor. 6:1-8) and to settle their disputes, like the ancient Hebrews, peaceably among their neighbors (Prv. 25:8-10). Although furnished as a guide to the just, the law was primarily directed to the lawless and the ungodly (1 Tm. 1:8-10). Christ himself had castigated the lawyers for taking away the key of knowledge, none other than that *caritas* which compels all men to live as brothers (Luke 11:52).

In view of such scriptural warnings, it was perhaps inevitable that lawyers, who were supposed to represent justice, should be among the first blamed for the imperfectability of mankind. Always at the center of worldly disputes, usually at the very hub of power, judges and advocates are the sitting ducks of social satire, a fate which they have never relinquished throughout the history of Western civilization. As Sir Morris Finer shrewdly observes, "Lawyers have never won a prize in the popularity stakes. It is a safe prediction that they never will. One has merely to speak of the *profession* of law, to detect that one has offended against the instinct that justice ought not to stand in need of the services of a middleman. The lawyer is an intruder into Eden; his presence an affront to the vision which men carry within them of a paradise lost, and hopefully to be regained, in which lambs and lions will congregate without specialist assistance. The philosophical practitioner of the law accepts the point. He acknowledges his role as victim of the yearning for a Golden Age, as a fomentor of that tension which is bound to arise between individuals' feeling for justice and society's need for the law."[2]

These timely words reflect admirably the refreshing spirit of self-criticism which has characterized the progress of legal reform in recent years; they also echo and substantiate a truth stated some years ago by F. W. Maitland, that "Englishmen have trusted the law; it were hardly too much too say that they have loved the law; but they have not loved and do not love lawyers."[3]

In these ideal terms, the achievement of justice is impossible because the

Golden Age, or paradise, lies outside of human experience, and prelapsarian perfection can only be conceived of through leaps of negative imagination, just as theologians can only describe God's being as infinite, unknowable, or immeasurable in contrast to the finite reality which circumscribes all human and physical life. Adam's innocence was not merely a state of blissful ignorance; it was a kind of knowledge which was unharmful (*innocens*), and the eating of the forbidden fruit introduced the acquisition of *knowledge* as we understand the term, although it also necessitated an ignorance of the truth which prevailed before the fall. Our brand of knowledge, therefore, obscures our vision of paradise and its meaning. If Adam did not know the meaning of evil, then the concept of justice as we understand it is meaningless in prelapsarian terms. If lambs and lions congregate peaceably, then we cannot actually think of them as lambs and lions, and we cannot understand perfection because it is essentially unhuman. In fact, the most exciting feature of Milton's *Paradise Lost* lies not in his explanation of perfection but in the poet's description of how Adam and Eve achieve selfhood, whereby they exchange their unobscured knowledge of the Deity for human personality. They are expelled from the Garden because they have discovered separate identities, not only from God but between themselves. In coping with their guilt, they learn the distinction between *mine* and *thine,* just as they must learn to share, thus laying the foundation for the formation of society.

Many writers have tried to reconstruct the ideal society and have been forced to take into their accounts the dangers inherent in ownership and property (*meum et tuum*). In his *Republic,* Plato surmounts the problem of personal property (tautologous phrase) by relegating it to the masses, the appetitive underbelly of society whose collective soul must be governed by the virtue of temperance. The guardians favor a communal existence by insisting that philosophy, the source of wisdom, and personal property are incompatible. Platonic otherworldliness had a natural appeal for the early Christians because it meshed with the Christian dictum to "sell all thou hast and follow Me," a precept which led to the rapid rise of monastic settlements dedicated to the principle of shared property (a contradiction in terms). At the beginning of the sixteenth century, Sir Thomas More combined these models in fashioning his Utopian society (the satirical antithesis of greed-torn Europe), in which all forms of personal property are abolished, and money is worthless except as a concession to foreign avarice. Obviously, if one considers such contemporary extravagance as the Field of the Cloth of Gold, the royal entertainments at Hampton Court, and the building of Nonsuch, the satire had little immediate impact in the real world. Fortunately, however, *Utopia* wielded a strong literary influence upon later writers like Montaigne, Bacon, and Swift, not to mention Utopians of far lesser ability.

Not least among these influences is More's treatment of the law. In part 1 of *Utopia,* the author provides a portrait of a typical contemporary lawyer whose conduct and opinions reflect More's contempt for professional rapacity and affectation. Insensitive to the plight of the poor, merciless in his persecution of petty criminals, contentious to the point of rudeness, this lawyer is so wrapped up in his legal forms and procedures, so afraid of losing a suit, that he cannot see the legal forest for the trees. He cannot, however, be simply dismissed as an innocuous bore because he epitomizes the worst aspects of early sixteenth-century legal practice. It is within the context of this representative lawyer's thinking that we may see why More, himself a brilliant and successful lawyer, designs a legal system so simple and straightforward for his Utopians that no serious threat of civil injustice exists in his ideal commonwealth. "Moreover," remarks Hythloday, who has just returned from Utopia, "they absolutely banish from their country all lawyers, who cleverly manipulate cases and cunningly argue legal points. They consider it is a good thing that every man should plead his own cause and say the same to the judge as he would tell his counsel. Thus there is less ambiguity and the truth is more easily elicited when a man, uncoached in deception by a lawyer conducts his own case and the judge skillfully weighs each statement, and helps untutored minds to defeat the false accusations of the crafty." The legal principles are based upon Platonic and scriptural sources. In his own career, however, More taught by precept and example rather than as an avid reformer of the bar.[4]

In his famous essay "On Experience," Montaigne, a magistrate with some experience in French civil law, echoes More's legal philosophy by attacking judicial and procedural complexities as yet another form of that kind of pedantry which he so heartily despised. He calls the Golden Age to witness and invokes the law of nature in his praise of King Ferdinand of Spain who, when he sent colonists to the West Indies, "wisely provided that no students of jurisprudence should accompany them, for fear that lawsuits might breed in this new world, this being by nature a science generating altercation and division; judging with Plato, that lawyers and doctors are a bad provision for a country."[5] Experience had taught Montaigne that many disputes are deliberately caused by lawyers who complicate issues chiefly for their own benefit by making the law so obscure that it cannot be understood by the common man. In England, too, the deliberate agitation of civil and criminal litigation (in the forms of barratry and maintenance) had been a constant source of national concern since the fourteenth century.[6] Humanistic weariness with continual civil turmoil may in part account for the literary creation of so many ideal, lawyerless societies in the later Tudor-Stuart period, such as Sidney's Arcadia, Shakespeare's Forest of Arden, Bacon's New Atlantis, or even Winstanley's Digger Colony at St. George's Hill, harmonious retreats from the chaos of the external world, settings in which evils can be isolated and examined as phenomenal.

Law has no real place in such bowers of retirement and universal accord. When it does intrude, as in Daniel's *The Queene's Arcadia,* the peace is shattered and the magic disappears. In this poem, the threat is posed by the arrival of Lincus the attorney and Alcon the quacksalver, who deliberately set out to "dissolve the frame and composition" of the ideal society. In the sheer absence of civil dissension, the attorney has nothing to do; he cannot make a profit out of perfection:

> ... these poore people of *Arcadia* here
> Are soone contented each man with his owne,
> As they desire no more, nor will be drawne
> To any contestation....
> ....
> But having here no matter whereupon
> To furnish reall actions, as elsewhere;
> No tenures, but a customary hold
> Of what they have from their progenitors
> Common, without individuitie;
> No purchasings, no contracts, no comerse,
> No politique comands, no services,
> No generall assemblies but to feast
> And to delight themselves with fresh pastimes;
> How can I hope that I shall ever thrive? [7]

Lincus's only recourse is to launch an all-out educational program to teach the Arcadians the meaning of personal property:

> Which now I seeke to doe, by drawing them
> To appr'hend of these proprieties
> Of *mine and thine,* and teach them to incroach
> And get them states apart, and private shares.
> (lines 1000-1003)

After some initial success, the intruders into this Eden are banished unceremoniously from Arcadia, this action being the only means of preserving the harmony and simplicity of the state.

The Arcadian theme is often introduced into darker and more sinister situations. In Shakespeare's *The Tempest,* for example, just before Ariel thwarts Antonio and Sebastian's plan to murder the sleeping Alonzo, Gonzalo describes what he would do if he were king of Prospero's island, in words which recall Montaigne's praise of King Ferdinand:

> I' the commonwealth I would by contraries
> Execute all things; for no kind of traffic

> Would I admit; no name of magistrate;
> Letters should not be known; riches, poverty,
> And use of service, none; contract, succession,
> Bourn, bound of land, tilth, vineyard, none;
> No use of metal, corn, or wine, or oil;
> No occupation; all men idle, all;
> And women too, but innocent and pure;
> No sovereignty—[8]

When Gonzalo further decides to ban all treason and felonies, the irony is clear, for the speech occurs only moments before the intended regicide swallows up all this finespun nonsense. As Robert Burton dryly remarks, "Utopian parity is a kind of government to be wished for rather than effected, *Respub. Christianopolitana,* Campanella's City of the Sun, and that new Atlantis, witty fictions...and Plato's community in many things is impious, absurd, and ridiculous."[9] Nevertheless, this more realistic view does not stop Burton from using the same motif as a medium of satirical commentary upon contemporary abuses and folly.

In most of these works, legal reform is associated with the need to abolish legal complexities and to simplify the language in which the law is expressed. In order to achieve universal respectability and to encourage civil obedience, government must rescue the law from the shamanism of its high priests who, in order to keep their power inviolate, enshroud the law in deepest mystery. Fulke Greville suggests in his *Monarchie* a complete revision and codification of the law as a means of preventing further corruption:

> Hence must their aphorisms which doe comprise
> The summe of law be published, and stil'd
> In such a common language as is pris'd
> And us'd abroad, not from the world exil'd;
>   Least being both in text, and language thrall,
>   They prove noe coynes for traffique generall.
>
> For is it meete that lawes which ought to bee
> Rules unto all men, showld rest knowne to few?
> Since then how can pow'rs soveraignitie
> Of universall justice beare a shew,
>   Reforme the judge, correct the advocate,
>   Who knowinge law alone commaunds the state?[10]

During the Commonwealth, religious Utopians took the myth of the golden age even more seriously and clamored for an abolition of the legal profession. Radical

Puritans such as the Diggers stressed Christ's moral condemnation of lawyers and his distrust for the sterility of rules without mutual faith and trust. Typical of this kind of criticism is Henry Robinson's *Certaine Proposals to a New Modelling of the Lawes* (1653), in which the reformer heaps scorn upon lawyers as "the most vaine, not onely unnecessary but mischievous, destructive to a common-wealth...their learning is but law-cheating, jugling, pocket-picking," and he proposes his new system "to make the dark mystery of the lawes...more practicable than cookery."[11]

Fortunately, not all proposals for legal reform were as inane as Robinson's. The common law survived intact into the Restoration and continued to supply authors with the inspiration for Utopian worlds such as the land of the Houyhnhnms in Swift's *Gulliver's Travels*. Swift certainly had More in mind when he devised the legal system of Brobdingnag, where the laws are written in brief sentences of never more than twenty-two words and are "expressed in the most plain and simple Terms, wherein those People are not Mercurial enough to discover above one Interpretation." Among the good giants, it is a capital offense to write commentaries on the law, and precedents are so few that their lawyers "have little Reason to boast of any extraordinary Skill in Pleading." All Gulliver's hosts express amazement at the rapacity of Europeans, and the Master Houyhnhnm can understand the Yahoo system of law only by a heroic leap of imagination.[12] Gulliver eventually returns to England having learned from experience that man is a fallen, imperfectible creature out of tune with the Hidden Law. If he is to regain his paradise, man must either cease to be human or, like Christian, leave his litigation in the city of Destruction.

Satire and the Law

In his autobiography, Anthony Trollope makes the point that "any writer in advocating a cause must do so after the fashion of an advocate, or his writing will be ineffective. He should take up one side and cling to that, and then he may be powerful. There should be no scruples of conscience. Such scruples make a man impotent for such work." This observation is particularly true for the satirist, as James Sutherland has emphasized.[13] The satirist is a prosecutor of social evils, who argues either for a traditional point of view or for a code of emerging values. He has a case to try for the public he represents and cannot be unduly concerned about the extenuating circumstances or the defendant's redeeming features. In presenting his lively image of the absurd, the satirist must exaggerate the proportions and the implications of the evils he wishes to indict. Likewise, as a literary judge, he bases his verdicts and reports upon clearly established codes of moral behavior, norms which have either been documented or customarily accepted time out of mind.

Like the lawyer, the satirist has a propensity for appealing to precedents, that is to conventions which have provided moral standards for centuries of experience. There is a similar predictability about both satirical and legal "types." The parasite will make friends with anyone for a meal, the wily servant is always deceiving his master in order to obtain favors for a romantic son, and the miles gloriosus brags his way out of many a fight. In legal literature, John Doe is the perpetual victim of brutal treatment and is "in despair of his life," Richard Roe is always running around with "swords, staves, knives, bows, and arrows," and the Reasonable Man, who appears in a bewildering multiplicity of civil suits, has never taken a risk of any kind for well over two hundred years. Many of these types have an amazing longevity and can be expected to re-emerge into new legal or literary settings until they have exhausted their purpose. Just as the common law depends upon clearly defined precedents and maxims, effective satire usually depends upon a set of readily accepted social norms. In law and satire alike, it is customarily the normative prescriptions which generate the body of precedents, which in turn govern judgments in individual cases or works. In both fields, the type retains its significance only as long as it embodies a set of readily recognized and conventional characteristics, all of which constitute its composite representation.

Likewise, in their earliest historical development, satire and law are similar in being highly formulaic and ritualistic. Just as the writs and assizes of the early common law are expressed in rigidly precise linguistic terms, so the earliest medieval satire is based upon conventions of a formulaic kind. For example, writs of trespass invariably follow the same basic pattern and use identical phrases, such as *contra pacem regis, cum vi et armis,* and *quare clausum fregit,* to signal a particular type of action. Similarly, the virtues and vices of medieval estates satire and venality satire are described in conventional terms and are recognizable because of their formulaic behavior, props, and language. Moreover, the language and forms in both fields develop in much the same way as the formulaic conventions are adapted to new needs, combine with new forms, and finally take on lives of their own. At law, for example, trespass is molded to other types of action such as debt, detinue, and negligence until each pursues its own development as a distinct action. In satire, the vices break away from their brethren, reappear in new settings, and combine with other types such as the wicked counselor, the braggart knight, or the late medieval vice, eventually to influence the creation of distinct characters like Shakespeare's Richard III, Falstaff, and Iago, or otherwise to provide the basic conventional features of the types found in seventeenth-century character books.

Modern lawyers are frequently told that they will achieve a better understanding of the law if they acquire a solid background in the history and development of the forms and actions of the common law. The student of satire may also obtain a clearer understanding of his subject by tracing the development of conventions and forms of satire through all their historical ramifications. Herein lies part of the significance of approaching specific characters, like the lawyer, from the standpoint of formulaic literary representations; for just as characters are typed, forming over the centuries immensely long and complicated genealogies, so are the plot situations in which these types find themselves embroiled. In satire, the least dramatic of all literary modes, the literary event or situation rarely arises purely from the character's internal motivation. In fact, the ritual process of satire reflects the adversary structure of legal procedure.[14] The satirist's chief skill is to weave these typical situations and patterns into endless variations and complications as they introduce the representational figure into new and particular cases. Like the lawyer, the satirist must also subdue ambiguity at all costs. The use of irony and innuendo must be reasonably clear while he permits the spirit of exaggeration of the trivial to run rampant.

Medieval Satire of the Law

Accustomed as we are to the highly topical and Latinate satire of the eighteenth century, we may experience some difficulty in appreciating the satire of the medieval period. We may also fail to recognize that later satire is often strongly influenced by the medieval tradition, as in the case of seventeenth-century character books and satirical drama. Influential critics like Sutherland, Hodgart, and Kernan either ignore medieval satire or pointedly suggest that medieval literature be excluded from the history of satire, despite the fact that medievalists have produced several useful books on the subject. Since such works as *Piers Plowman* and Gower's *Vox Clamantis* do not conform to the principles of Augustan satire, they are relegated to the level of mere preaching, a problem no doubt exacerbated by Owst's remarkable study of the influence of the sermon upon Middle English literature.[15] Chaucer's poetry is often excepted from such adverse criticism because of the poet's superior comic sense and so-called realism—his need to instruct does not outrun his desire to entertain. Although there may be some truth to such verdicts, it is dangerous for the modern reader to assume that the medieval audience was not delighted by their morally-oriented literature. How else can we explain the apparent popularity of sober works like Dan Michael's *Ayenbite of Inwit* and *Cursor Mundi?* As Jill Mann and John A. Yunck have conclusively shown, it is difficult to appreciate the satire of Chaucer, Gower, and Langland without knowing something of the traditions of estates and venality satire.[16] Close reading of this essential background literature discloses a dual genealogy of ideal and vicious character types, who either represent or defy the accepted norms of Christian and professional morality. These conventional representations are drawn from all levels of medieval society and, within the twofold scheme, portray moral antitheses according to a wide range of moral precepts. In this gallery of types, one finds ideal and vicious knights, friars, parsons, and laborers, always unambiguously opposed. Chaucer's innovation, perhaps the chief source of his "realism," was to mix the characteristics of good and evil types in varying degrees, so that the majority of his Canterbury pilgrims are neither entirely good nor completely evil. By mixing good and evil representations, Chaucer makes his pilgrims seem human and fully realized psychologically.

In regard to satire of the legal profession, however, one notices an absence of firmly established morality portraiture. Members of the third estate, lawyers had only recently emerged as a separate professional class, particularly in England where the judiciary had been dominated until the late thirteenth century by high churchmen and where so many legal offices were held by laymen rather than by professionals.[17] It was not until this time, when the estates tradition was already well established, that we find anything like a fully-fledged bar, providing pleaders (*narratores, contours,* or *serviantes*) for the central courts while becoming the sole source of judicial appointments. Thus, the portraits of lawyers in such works as *The Canterbury Tales, Piers Plowman, Mom and Sothsegger,* and *London Lickpenny,* although heavily influenced by estates and venality satire, tend to be based more accurately upon contemporary criticisms of the legal profession. Rudolf Kirk, for example, has counted over fifty separate legal terms in the C-text of *Piers Plowman* and several other allusions to contemporary legislation such as the Statutes of Laborers.[18]

In larger moral terms, however, law satire imitates established tradition in being extremely generalized. The vicious lawyer, like the evil friar or the tyrannical knight, may be guilty of any of the seven deadly sins. Otherwise, lawyers are criticized for real legal faults, such as pandering to the rich, ignoring the *querelae* of the poor, prolonging or delaying litigation, padding fees, and engaging in a greedy scramble for lands.[19] To Gower, for example, the lawyer's besetting sin is avarice: "I therefore direct my writings in particular to those whom the sin of avarice leads astray, and not to others. Under the cloak of law hides cleverness, whereby a law without justice daily devotes itself to carrying out its wishes somehow. When lawyers can twist this kind of law, they transmute the justice begotten of their own words. Everything is tinted in the guise of justice, whereby their sly administration of justice brings them the more profit. They care not in what way a case is just or unjust, but that it be rich in returns for them."[20]

Despite their presence in formal allegorical works, many of these lawyers seem convincingly real, like the "lordliche" crew which follows upon the train of Lady Meed in *Piers Plowman.* Our predisposition urges us to cherish these glimpses of medieval reality, but we must exercise some caution, for the life and bustle of these passages may have provoked an entirely different response from the medieval audience. What often appears to the modern reader as wit and charm would be regarded as moral depravity by the sterner moralists of Langland's time. No matter how engaging, cogent, and colorful these characters may appear to us, they must be judged ultimately in terms of the ideal conduct which determined the medieval understanding of their behavior. In this morally-oriented literature, the ideal figure or value always shines through the disguise, and one must read these satirical pieces as parody (*parodia*), in which the ideal paradigm is so secure and firmly believed that it is always the vicious character who reaps the contempt and scorn of the medieval reader. Thus, in legal satire, evil judges like Appius, Pilate, or the magistrates who threaten Susannah must be set over and against such sublime and unambiguously ideal figures as Daniel, Solomon, or even the Christ of the last judgment. To some extent, all trial scenes bear a twofold relationship, first to the diabolically inspired indictment of Christ and second to the inevitable judgments of the day of doom, constant themes in both mystery and morality drama.

While it is possible to find adverse judgments of the law in early medieval literature, especially in monastic chronicles, it is not until the late Ricardian period that we notice a marked increase in the flow of anti-law satire.[21] Several reasons may account for the significant upswing in satirical attacks upon the law. The Black Death and the Peasants' Revolt (1381) had ushered in a period of economic change which struck at the very roots of feudal society, all this coinciding with the phenomenal growth of the middle classes. Although the value system associated with feudalism remained largely intact, it was, nevertheless, the legal profession which introduced the most dramatic social changes and which fostered the growth of mercantile enterprise, not only in the expansion of commerce but also in the all-important distribution of landed wealth.[22] In fact, much of the turmoil of the fifteenth century resulted from the fact that the church and the nobility realized the dangers of the gradual loosening of the tenurial system, and had to fight to preserve their ancient privileges in the land. The ensuing disorder inspired a great wave of scathing satire directed at the legal profession which found it virtually impossible to contain the social and political chaos which they had partly initiated. As members of the burgeoning middle class, lawyers had greatly prospered under the changing system and had vested interests of their own to protect. Consequently, the legal profession— from the judges, serjeants, and barristers of the central courts down to the lower ranks of attorneys and clerks—came in for ferocious satirical abuse. John Wycliff's attacks seem typical enough, when he upbraids these "false procouratouris of sathanas" because they "norischen pledynge and debate among men for to have a veyn name and wynnen hem a litil worldly stynkynge muk with goddis curs" and because they "forbarien pore men" and "make many doseyns to forswaren hem on the boke to get hem self thank or wynnynge."[23] As we shall see, the satirical representations of lawyers are largely based upon such extraliterary sources.

Complaints such as these, however, must not be construed to mean that satirists condemned the value system upon which the law was founded or that they were promulgating new democratic principles of justice. On the contrary, Wycliff actually supported the common law, and critics like Gower were merely attempting to shore up and preserve an ethical program already embodied in the law. As V. J. Scattergood observes of the fifteenth-century literature of social protest, "Despite the completeness of their attacks and despite the very real feelings of frustration and dissatisfaction evident in them, these poems were not revolutionary. They contain no proposals for overthrowing and renewing the decadent society they deplore. In spirit they are conservative. Though they criticize contemporary society, they unfailingly endorse, either overtly or by implication, those assumptions and values upon which it was based.... Contemporary evils are defined here as a reversal of an accepted set of social and moral values, and the poet's certainty of the rightness of these values sharpens his sense of how far contemporary society has deviated from them."[24] Lurid descriptions of legal corruption and severe criticism of lawyers should not, then, be taken as proof that satirists felt any real disaffection for the law per se. Peter Idley's poetical *Instructions to His Son* (c. 1450) paints a rather gloomy picture of legal fraud and deceit, yet Idley still encourages his son to enter the profession as an honorable career.[25] The positive thrust of Idley's criticism of the law is to demonstrate what a good lawyer must do by confronting the reader with the temptations he must overcome.

Transition to the Renaissance

Even though similar criticisms of lawyers are voiced in different periods, it is essential to assess any piece of law satire within a dual framework of literary and historical commentary, in order to determine how a particular representation changes through time. In the transition from the medieval period to the Renaissance (wherever one sets the precise limits of these periods), one immediately recognizes many topical and thematic continuities in law satire. In an excellent survey of the lawyer's reputation in the popular literature of the early Tudor period. E. W. Ives lists six major grievances constantly voiced against the profession, in addition to the overriding consideration of avarice: provocation of litigation for profit, delay of proceedings, judicial susceptibility to the influence of the rich and powerful, the charging of excessive fees, the perversion of justice through misuse of procedural technicalities, and the general complaint that there are too many lawyers. Quite correctly, Ives suggests that these common laments stem from medieval literature. Every one of these criticisms, for example, can be found in the works of Gower and Wycliff, or even more archetypally in the Middle English *Book of Vices and Virtues*.[26] Ives is also partially correct in attributing much of this satire to moral idealism and ignorance of the law, and in deploring the paucity of unbiased evidence.

However, as already indicated, the satirist is always biased and morally right. He is a prosecutor of vice and must ignore scruples if, as Trollope warns, he wishes to be effective. As for ignorance, one must also remember that many satirists during this period, like Gower, Idley, More, and George Gascoigne, were either lawyers themselves or closely associated with the law, and it is virtually impossible to verify the full extent of legal corruption by means of documentary proofs. While there is much exaggeration in the satirical representation of lawyers, and while the characterization is indeed typical, the popular criticism of lawyers is also frequently based upon specific legal abuses in specific courts and thus reflects issues of genuine contemporary concern. Idley decries abuses in the local administration of the law and the tampering with juries. More's Hythloday inveighs against professional indifference for the poor, the severity of the criminal law, and the spread of enclosures. Other writers like Henry Brinklow, Philip Stubbes, and Thomas Starkey attack abuses in the administration of feudal incidents of wardship and marriage.[27] In other words, the stereotyped representation is inevitably drawn into the orbit of contemporary political concerns. Furthermore, if legal corruption was not a matter of vital professional importance, why then do we find so many documented attempts to impose sanctions upon dishonest lawyers, such as those who accepted fees for the bribing of juries and witnesses, those who faced actions upon the case *pro deceptione* for ambidextry (taking fees from plaintiff and defendant), and those (usually attorneys and solicitors) who were charged in the Court of Star Chamber for various kinds of malpractice?[28] There seems little reason to believe that so much adverse criticism of the legal profession arose in a vacuum of justifiable causes.

After 1550 the representation of lawyers becomes considerably more complex. Although medieval portraiture survives in the creation of vicelike figures, the satirical typology is amplified and modified not only by classical and continental literary influences but also by new developments within the socio-legal framework. Representations of lawyers adopt certain characteristics of the Latin *advocatus* of classical drama, not to mention the deeper studies of the type, like Cleandro in Ariosto's *I Suppositi* and Giansimone in Grazzini's *La Sibilla.* Cleandro seems fairly representative of the type. His social preeminence reflects the tremendous prestige of the civil law taught in Italian universities, and he prides himself on the superiority of his wisdom, his great wealth, and his eloquence, while assuming some of the features of the pedant and of the *senex amans.*[29]

It would be a mistake, however, to overestimate the significance of these foreign influences in the works of English authors. The moral flavor of medieval satire remains a deep and constant influence upon all types of satirical literature, like the character books, epigrams, verse satire, and especially the drama. Perhaps the most important and instructive portrait of a lawyer in all

Renaissance drama is the character of Ignoramus in Ruggle's Latin play (of the same title) performed at Cambridge University in 1614.[30] Even though this comedy is based upon Giambattista della Porta's *La Trappolaria,* and ultimately upon the *Pseudolis* of Plautus, the characterization of Ignoramus owes nothing to these sources, for the legal plot is grafted on to Porta's main plot. Ignoramus's given name, Ambidexter, provides a sufficient clue to his true identity, and his first entrance upon stage betrays his genealogy. His opening speeches are sprinkled with exclamations such as "phy, phy" and "ho, ho," which echo the typical first appearance of the vice figures of morality drama. We can imagine Ignoramus as having a beet-red complexion as he prances ludicrously around the stage exclaiming, "O chaud, chaud: precor Deum non meltavi meum pingue" (O hot, hot, I pray God I have not melted my lard) and "Meltor, Dulman, meltor. Rubba me cum towallio, rubba" (I melt, Dulman, I melt. Rub me with a towel, rub), lines no doubt intended to cast our minds back to types like red-faced Herod and ranting Pilate.[31] Such characters as Ignoramus differ from the early vice figures mainly by being given a local habitation and a name.

While their literary roots are apparent, the lawyers of Renaissance satire also reflect new preoccupations and new grounds for criticism. The topics of ignorance and pedantry stem not only from continental *advocati* but also from a growing humanistic concern for standards of legal education and the purity of language. So much is made of the linguistic barbarities of common law language, in fact, that I would add this topic to the list of chief complaints devised by Dr. Ives.[32] English law suffered from a peculiar defect in the eyes of humanistic scholars since it was based upon a combination of two dead languages: Law French and Latin. Law French, a species of Anglo-Norman, much decayed, was no longer understood except by those trained at the Inns of Court. In fact, neither language was capable of comprehensively expressing the newest developments in legal practice. Therefore, if medieval Latin or Law French did not furnish the appropriate word, a weird neologism would often be coined (often paired with an English word and an *anglice* or *vocatus*). Sometimes the English word would appear in the middle of the French or Latin passage, or, what is worse, would be given Latin inflections. Ruggle's *Ignoramus* pokes fun at this practice with such amusing coinages as "warrantizabo," "transi-tempus," and "Gownos, Silkcotos, Kirtellos, et Petticotos." Although the satire of legal language exaggerates this problem, practically everyone knows the story of the condemned prisoner who, when sentenced by Chief Justice Richardson at the Wiltshire Assizes, *"ject un Brickbat a le dit Justice que narrowly mist."*[33] University scholars were obviously disturbed by the macaronic jumble of law language. Even Sir Thomas Smith in his great eulogy of the common law, *De Republica Anglorum,* feels compelled to state his reservations about the barbarous quality of Law-Latin. The following comment by Sir Francis Bacon may reflect the uneasiness experienced by lawyers who had been educated at the university: "Wherein this phrase (*ad opus & usum*) and the Words (*ad opus*) is a barbarous phrase, and like enough to be in the penning of some Chaplaine that was not much past his Grammar, where he had found *Opus & usus,* coupled together, and that they did governe an Ablative case, as they do indeed since this Statute, for they take away the Land and put them into a conveyance."[34]

Renaissance law satire also retains another significant feature of earlier professional criticism; rarely, if ever, does satire in this period touch upon personalities. Occasionally, one discovers a direct reference to a historical figure, such as a mention of William Shareshull in *Wynnere and Wastoure,* or the veiled reference to Thomas Pynchbeck in Chaucer's *General Prologue* ("ther koude no wight pynche at his writyng"), and the obvious jibes against Lord Chancellor Wolsey in Skelton's "Why Come Ye Not to Court?" By and large, however, satirists avoided explicit name-calling during the Middle Ages and the early Renaissance. Beginning in the early seventeenth century, in spite of the ominous possibility of Star Chamber censures, there is an increasing propensity for particularized satire of contemporary lawyers. Much of this satire is deliberately anonymous and was distributed in manuscript form, and usually this kind of criticism is leveled at political targets and does not necessarily reflect upon the profession as a whole. Ruggle's *Ignoramus,* which was never published in the author's lifetime, is aimed at Francis Brackyn, Recorder of Cambridge; and, because it was championed by James I, the comedy became the center of a great controversy involving Lord Chief Justice Coke, the Inns of Court, and the universities.[35] According to one source, the satirical comedy was performed upon several occasions both at Cambridge and Royston, and perhaps at Whitehall, "with great applause":

> At one of which times the King cried out Treason, Treason. And being asked what was the matter, said, he believed the Author, and the Actors together had a design...to make him laugh himself to death. Another time when the King was seated, and expected the scholars to perform, he was surprised with the sound of a horn and the appearance of a Post-boy, who said that Ignoramus was prepared to play his part, but that none of the Lawyers would lend him a gown to act in. Ah, said the King (who was deceived and took the Scholar for a real post-boy) this is a plot of Cukes! (meaning the Ld. C. Justice Coke). But if Cuke won't let the Lawyers lend him a Gown, by my Saul, man, he shall lend him his own. This speech of the King put the audience into an exceeding merry humour, and the Play went on.[36]

The post-boy in this report, of course, is the *Puer Veredarius* of the *Prologus Posterior* of *Ignoramus,* written for the second performance of the play in 1615. Stories of this kind must have infuriated the embattled Coke, then not only High Steward of Cambridge but also engaged in an unrelenting struggle against Ellesmere, Bacon, and the royal prerogative. His reaction to *Ignoramus* is reported by John Chamberlain: "On Saturday last the King went to Cambridge to see the play *Ignoramus,* which has so nettled the lawyers that they are almost out of all patience, and the Lord Chief Justice, both openly at the King's Bench and diverse other places, hath galled and glanced at scholars with much bitterness, and there be diverse Inn of Court men have made rhymes and ballads against them, which they have answered sharply enough."[37] Chamberlain's following remarks probably identify the author's chief intention, which was to write a more general type of satire with a barb or two thrust in the direction of Brackyn: "And to say truth it was a scandal taken rather than given, for what profession is there wherein some particular persons may not be justly taxed without imputation to the whole? But it is an old saying, *conscius ipse tibi,* and they are too particular to think themselves so *sacrosancti* that they may not be touched."[38] Not everyone in this turbulent age was so levelheaded and impartial as Chamberlain.

Nevertheless, it is clear that *Ignoramus* heralded a new era of legal satire which indulged itself in nearly two centuries of increasingly personal attacks upon the legal profession. Certainly during the Stuart and Commonwealth periods, eminent lawyers were far from *sacrosancti,* especially those who found themselves embroiled in such heated issues as monopolies, ship money, and the continuing battle of the royal prerogative. Much of this satire, like Massinger's treatment of Sir Giles Mompessen and Sir Francis Michel in *A New Way to Pay Old Debts,* or the Restoration lampoons directed at judges like Bradshaw, Scroggs, and Jeffreys, was well deserved. Other satirical attacks, such as the Commonwealth diatribes aimed at royalist judges, are decidedly partisan and political and, thus, stray beyond the parameters of the representation of the common lawyer. The chief interest of this study is satire of a more general nature, however, and it therefore concentrates on the common law rather than issues of a political nature.

2

Satire, Legal Education, and the Inns

Now Causey to the Temple went,
To study Law was his intent;
And he, the Counsellor to put on,
For twelve whole terms must eat their mutton;
Quoth he, I've frequently been told
That Midas turn'd all things to gold,
And from this precedent I draw,
They turn their Mutton into Law,
Then if the Law be in the Meat,
He most must know who most can eat.
　　　Anon., "Causidicus, A Poetical Lash" (1779)

AT THE END OF THE eighteenth century, according to the familiar joke, it was said that law students at the Inns of Court could eat their way to the bar. In other words, legal education had returned full circle to its medieval beginnings when apprentice lawyers learned from attendance at court or from senior lawyers and when the Inns were merely places of residence, with no formal program of education.

In its earliest phases, the common law operated in rather direct fashion and did not require the service of professional lawyers. The doing of right usually involved a royal command in the form of a writ issued by the Chancery, local action by the sheriff or king's representative, and a trial in which the defendant was expected to respond accurately to rigidly worded formulae. Questions of right could be decided by ordeal, battle, compurgation of oath-helpers, or by an inquisition in which a presenting jury rendered *veredicta* based upon their personal knowledge of the facts. Cases were never tried on their full merits but were narrowed procedurally to the determination of particular issues, each issue central to the entire dispute. The litigant could be represented at the trial by an *attornatus,* a person officially authorized to act in the place of the litigant or to submit essoins, legally acceptable excuses for failure to appear in propria persona.[1] Since trial (joining issue) preceded proof, and since proof appealed to the supernatural intervention of God (as in trial by battle or ordeal), there was little in the way of complicated pleading.

During the reign of Henry II and continuing until the reign of Edward I, however, the central courts underwent a period of intensive growth and rapid change brought about by a great proliferation of *de cursu* writs. The increasing complication of the writ system, with the gradual development of special pleading and the introduction of new statutory legislation, made it impossible for individuals to conduct their own affairs in the royal courts. The legal profession, therefore, arose as a necessary response to the growing complexity of the law. Historically, the professional attorneys came first and were usually enrolled by specific courts. Their job was to prepare cases for litigation and later to submit briefs to the pleaders. The order of serjeants, who held a monopoly of pleading in the Court of Common Pleas, seems firmly established by the third quarter of the thirteenth century, while the barristers, originally known as apprentices, sprang into prominence during the fourteenth century and shared the pleading responsibilities in Kings Bench and the Exchequer of Pleas. The solicitors, who managed litigation among several courts, cannot be said to have arrived as a professional class until the middle of the fifteenth century, although a few large landowners employed men who earlier fulfilled the managerial functions of solicitors.

Even in the absence of full and accurate information, the story of the rise and development of the new profession provides a fascinating chapter of medieval history: of how the first students crowded into the inns along Fleet Street, Holborn, and the Strand; how they formed societies of barristers and attorneys; and how, in the absence of textbooks, they laboriously compiled their own collections of writs, rules for pleading, and the case records which later blossomed into the remarkable Year Books.[2] It was probably not until much later, near the end of the Ricardian period, that the fuller curriculum of the Inns was introduced, including the Lent and Autumn Readings and the staging of mock trials (moots and bolts).[3]

The picture of legal life in England becomes much clearer in the Chaucerian period. It is even believed on the basis of doubtful evidence that Chaucer himself attended the Inns of Court. Actually, his poetry reveals no particular penchant for legal terms, although his portrait of the Man of Law in *The Canterbury Tales* depicts a lively representation of a fourteenth-century serjeant, as well as furnishing a moral exemplum.[4] A member of an elite group, the royally appointed serjeants, the Man of Law represents the flower of legal learning. The acme of competence, he knows the substance of cases and statute law going back to the time of William I. His legal writing and his pleadings are flawless, and he is naturally blessed with a full and busy practice. We see him at the Parvys, the porch of St. Paul's, drumming up business and giving legal advice, and, because he has been appointed "by pleyn commissioun" to ride the assize circuits, he may soon look forward to promotion to the bench.[5] Chaucer does not heap the derision upon this successful man that he may have received from moralists like Langland and Gower. All the same, glimmering through the complex surface of this portrait, a faint suspicion insinuates itself that this lawyer's gaze is riveted almost myopically upon purely worldly matters. One begins to wonder if his acquisition of landed estates, all fee simple "in effect," has not resulted from the misuse of his remarkable talents. Attired in his coif, his motley coat, and his silk-striped girdle, he appears to us mainly in terms of externals, details which might be interpreted, within the context of the pilgrimage, as somewhat equivocal. Has he not, like his fellow pilgrims, set out on a journey to the New Jerusalem? Of what use, then, is his skill in human dealings if it has been solely directed toward the achievement of worldly prosperity? For the medieval audience, the moral values need not have been openly stated; they were universally understood. Chaucer merely leaves unsaid what writers like Langland make crystal clear. The moral lesson, then, of this portrait is that persons endowed with great intellectual talent must employ their skill and wisdom unselfishly for the improvement of human relationships. Innocent III, for example, makes this argument in his condemnation of lawyers who sacrifice the poor to the rich and who distort justice for their own greedy purposes, and to reinforce the point he quotes Matthew 10:8: "Freely give what you have received."[6] Richard de Bury, in another context, condemns legal studies as a kind of *geologia* (a worldly study), not worthy to be ranked among the genuine arts and sciences. Legal study, he declares, detracts from the contemplation of the scriptures while inevitably encouraging contention, avarice, and duplicity. Wycliff also condemns the study of worldly law because it threatens to replace the law of the gospels.[7] Human law must seek to establish a charitable relationship with the divine law; otherwise, the true end of man's being will be forgotten as he becomes engulfed in purely secular concerns.

Lawyers were probably far more devout than the poets and preachers would have us believe. Sir John Fortescue, writing in the Lancastrian period, recommends the scriptures as necessary preparation for students of the law: "Wherefore the Justyces after they have taken their reflection, doo passe and bestowe all the residue of the days in the studye of the lawes, in readynge holy Scripture, and usynge other kynde of contemplacion at their pleasure. So that theire life may seeme more contemplative then active."[8] If John Manningham's

Middle Temple diary is at all representative of life at the Inns at the close of the sixteenth century, then we cannot dismiss common lawyers as irreligious because within the space of two years Manningham amassed notes (some very extensive) on no fewer than forty-two sermons. A half-century later, Chief Justice Sir Matthew Hale devised for himself a rigorous program of moral rules to live by, with considerable portions of time set aside daily for prayer and meditation.[9] The Inns, however, attracted all sorts and conditions of men, as a reading of the Black Books reveals.

Much has been written about the origins and development of legal education at the Inns of Court, but we are unfortunate in possessing no records earlier than the beginning of the fifteenth century.[10] At first, the Inns where chiefly places of residence, as the word suggests, and were patronized by law students for their convenient location halfway between the city of London and the royal courts of Westminster. As the numbers of students increased, inns and private residences were rented for the exclusive use of student-lawyers, and rules were formulated for the government of those who maintained chambers there. The barristers occupied the Inns of Court (Lincoln's Inn, Gray's Inn, and the Inner and the Middle Temples) while the attorneys established residence at the Inns of Chancery (Clifford's, Furnival's, Clement's, Barnard's, Davies', Lyon's, Staple Inn, and New Inn), each of which became loosely affiliated with one of the superior Inns. In fact, barristers from the Inns of Court were appointed as readers at the lower Inns. During the formative years, the Inns of Chancery could even send their most promising students to their affiliated senior Inns.[11]

Education at all the Inns was practical rather than theoretical. The Inns of Chancery were so named because their principal study was the system of Chancery writs which determined the forms and actions. Such knowledge was not only vital for attorneys and the clerks of court, but it was also useful for those preparing for entrance to the superior Inns. Education at the Inns of Court was not rigidly formal and included private study, attendance at court, pleading conducted in moots and bolts, and attendance at the Lent and Autumn readings. The readings, delivered by recently appointed serjeants, invariably dealt with the interpretation of statutes, or selected chapters within statutes. Until the early sixteenth century, it was customary to deliver readings only upon the old statutes (pre-Edward III), following what appears to be a fairly regular historical sequence. The junior student, the inner barrister, was always the passive recipient of the learning and skill of the senior members: the utter barristers, who had received the call to the bar, and the benchers who sat at the head table and who superintended the social and educational life of the Inns. Since calls to the bar and appointment to the order of serjeants were strictly limited, even the most talented student might spend many years (eight to ten, or even longer) before attaining the highest successes the Inns afforded, and there were many who preferred, because of lucrative practices, to serve as attorneys (although this trend became increasingly frowned upon) or as practicing barristers who simply did not want to become serjeants.

The Inns of Court not only served, therefore, as a kind of third university but also as an important center of social, political, and diplomatic training. According to E. W. Ives, "Most Englishmen of Shakespeare's day saw the Inns as finishing schools for gentlemen."[12] They were great centers of culture, around which much of the intellectual and fashionable life of London flourished. However, it was this larger stress upon the social functions of the Inns which ultimately led to a weakening of their educational system.[13] Many of the students were merely residents who had no intention of pursuing legal careers. Some occupied chambers only to remain close to friends in the profession and others regarded a social connection with an Inn of Court as a likely avenue to political advancement. In spite of all the possible distractions from the primary task of legal education, the Inns, however, did maintain a vigorous and highly effective program throughout the Tudor era and well into the seventeenth century, although many of the outstanding lawyers of the time, such as Plowden, Coke, Popham, and Bacon, could also claim some preparation at either Oxford or Cambridge.

For the purposes of this study, it is crucial to recognize the outstanding contribution made by the Inns to the literary vitality of the late sixteenth century. Outside the universities, the Inns provided the greatest impetus to the sudden outburst of literary activity in the age of Elizabeth. University drama and poetry tended to be conservative, stuffy, and pedantic, and it was only after they had been released from the stifling atmosphere of academe that the university wits helped to spark the great renaissance of the 1580s. Clearly, then, their wit needed the kind of audience which only the third university could provide. Also, we must not forget that many great writers emerged from the ranks of those who lived in and around the Inns of Court, which furnished a more sophisticated public which demanded excellence and encouraged the creation of new dramatic forms.

As A. W. Green has shown, the Inns were often in the vanguard of dramatic experimentation, not only in the staging of lavish entertainments and masques but also in offering dramatists the opportunity of creating new forms.[14] Norton and Sackville's *Gorboduc,* acted at the Inner Temple in 1561, is generally regarded as the earliest genuinely English tragedy, dealing with British rather than classical or biblical history.[15] Gascoigne's *The Supposes* (1565) introduced Italian comedy to the English stage while the translations of Seneca by Newton and Heywood, and Hughes's *The Misfortunes of Arthur* (1588), initiated in the 1580s the vogue for tragedy in the Senecan vein. The Inns also provided an audience for those playwrights like Shakespeare who wrote mainly for the popular stage. *The Comedy of Errors, Twelfth Night,* and *Troilus and Cressida* are among the plays performed before the lawyers. It was also the legal profession which promoted the fashion for satirical comedy in the 1590s, not to mention the urbanity, wit, and savagery of the verse satire written at the turn of the century.[16] During this period, Marston, Donne, Guilpin, Hoskyns, Richard and Thomas Middleton, Thomas Overbury, and Sir John Davies were all residents at the Inns of Court. Not all the literary effusions of the lawyers, of course, can lay claim to greatness. Inferior productions such as the sonnet sequence *Zepheria* (1594) merit the ridicule of literati like Donne in "Satire II" and John Davies in his "Gulling Sonnets," and many doggerel Ovidian love elegies have mercifully passed into oblivion.[17]

After the great flowering of the Elizabethan-Jacobean era, the literary associations of the Inns suffered a remarkable decline throughout the remaining years of the seventeenth century. True, a few poets and dramatists like Carew, Ford, Denham, Suckling, and Butler joined the societies for fashion's sake, but they did not produce their best work during their brief stays at the Inns. As W. R. Prest justly observes, the only poets of any note who were full-time members during the Caroline period, such as Wither and May, were decidedly third-rate. Thomas Randolph seems well justified in his mockery of the sterility of their poetic efforts when he muses

> each day I'le write an Elegy,
> And in as lamentable Poetry,
> As any Inns of Court-man, that hath gone
> To buy an Ovid with a Littleton.[18]

The lawyer-poet becomes a conventional figure of amusement in seventeenth-century satire. As Oldfox in Wycherley's *The Plain-Dealer* dryly remarks, "*Appolo* and *Littleton* never lodge in a head together." In the same play, Manly is the defendant in a lawsuit for "advising a Poet to leave off Writing, and turn Lawyer, because he is dull, and impudent, and sayes or writes nothing now, but by Precedent."[19] His lawyer seems not to notice the insult.

Beginning from the early Jacobean period, a major share of the adverse criticism suffered by the legal world may be directly attributed to the gradual and steady decline in the standards of education at the Inns, not to mention the growing rivalry which arose between the Inns and the universities. In turn, this particular social development reflects itself, as we shall see, in the literary representation of lawyers during this period.

University criticism of the legal profession was prompted by a multiplicity of causes, and it would be difficult to pinpoint them because of the variety of political and religious loyalties of individual colleges. Clare Hall, Cambridge, for instance, was openly royalist and latitudinarian, whereas Trinity tended to favor the Puritan cause and the strategy of Parliament, yet both sides might have harsh things to say about lawyers: the Puritans from the standpoint of morality and higher law and the royalists in support of the royal prerogative, and both sides when it came to humanistic ideals of education such as the purity of classical versus Law Latin. Whatever the particular set of causes, seventeenth-century literature is saturated with derogatory comments about the quality of education received at the Inns of Court. Typical of these sentiments is Falso's statement in Middleton's *The Phoenix* (1607), "You see I have been a scholar in my time, though I'm a justice now." A similar opinion is expressed in Jonson's *The Poetaster* (1601): "Why the *law* makes a man happy, without respecting any other merit: a simple scholar, or none at all may be a lawyer." Ruggle's *Ignoramus* entertains a deep disdain for his *"Universitans,"* the scholarly Musaeus, and tries to achieve a measure of revenge against the academic world by ridiculing Musaeus but betrays his own stupidity with every remark he makes.[20] Webster echoes these sentiments and puts the shoe on the other foot when the learned Ariosto in *The Devil's Law-Case* scolds the ignorant attorney Sanitonella:

> The Devil take such Fees,
> And all such Suits i'th tayle of them; see the slave
> Has writ false Latine: sirrah Ignoramus,
> Were you ever at the Universities?[21]

As Parkhurst observes in his prologue to the king, written for the Whitehall production of *Ignoramus* in 1662, "Tis a Rule predestin'd by the Fates, / Lawyers and Schollars to be Disparats."[22] Even lawyers who attended the universities often expressed, in their private memoirs and reflections, their disapprobation and dismay at the quality of life and study at the Inns, comparing the harshness and barbarity of legal books unfavorably to "the fresh fragrant flowers of divine poesie and morall philosophy" which had occupied their hours at the universities. However, as W. R. Prest cautions, "Entrants from the universities who had imbibed the prejudices of clerical, classical dons were of course likely to be biased against the law from the start."[23]

Numerous reasons can be assigned to explain the decline in standards of legal education. Perhaps because of their continuing reputation for dissolute living, the Inns could no longer be highly regarded as finishing schools for gentlemen. As great centers of fashion and culture, it was only natural, in the absence of firm disciplinary controls and rigid admissions standards, that the Inns should attract the hangers-on and the wastrels who became proverbially known as Inns-a-Court fantastiques. As early as 1584, George Whetstone, in his glowing tribute to the Inns in *A Mirour for Magestrates of Cyties,* had warned students to employ their time wisely and avoid the temptations cast in their path, for, "by reason of Dicyng-howses, and other Alectives to unthriftinesse, the good father, which is at a charge, to make his Sonne a Lawier, to do his Countrey service, throughe the loosenesse of the sonne (many times) spendeth his money to the undooying of his posterytie." Later satire abounds with criticism of the lawless and lascivious conduct of law students, in which it appears that Whetstone's worst fears were realized under the Stuarts. To Overbury, the Inns-of-Court man is all externals, bad grammar, and overconfidence induced by heavy drinking.[24] Francis Lenton pillories their ignorance and lack of attention to legal studies, which are abandoned for all manner of vain pleasures:

> When he aspires once to be a Reveller, he then reveales himselfe to the full, and when he should bee mooting in the Hall, he is perhaps mounting in the Chamber, as if his father had only sent him to Cut Capers, and turne in the Ayre till his braines be adled, and make things meerely for ornament, matters of speciall use. His Recreations and loose expence of time, are his only studies (as Plaies, Dancing, Fencing, Taverns, Tobacco), and Dalliance, (which if it be with Time, is irrevocable) and are the alluring baits of ill disposed extravagants. He is roaring when hee should be reading, and feasting when he should be fasting, for his Friday-night supper doth usually equalize his weekely Commons, and it's to bee feared, he will exceed two meales in the weeke besides, with lac't Mutton, for whosoe're payes for his Comons, hee'l fall aboord. He is a youth very apt to bee wrought upon at first entrance, and there are Fishers of purpose for such young fry.[25]

The drama of this period provides an occasional glimpse into the low life associations of the Inns of Court, as in the capers of Plotwell, Newcut, and Bright in Jasper Mayne's *The Citie Match,* in which the Templars move with ease and familiarity among bawds, taverners, usurers and prostitutes.[26] The venal Throte in Barrey's *Ram-Alley* boasts of his sexual adventures during his days at the Inns of Court, as he lays his plot to carry off the wench Frances to be married at St. Giles in the Field:

> The time has beene when scarce an honnest women,
> much lesse a wench could passe an Inne of court,
> But some of the fry would have beene dooing
> With her: I knew the day when Shreds a Taylor,
> Coming once late by an Inne of Chancerie,
> Was laid along, and mufled in his cloake,
> His wife tooke in, Stycht up, turned out againe,
> And he perswaded all was but in iest.[27]

In Middleton's *Father Hubburd's Tales,* the ploughman describes how his young landlord is utterly ruined, first by conveying his landed estates away for money and then by losing all his money in ordinaries and dicing houses. The young man recuperates a part of his fortune by becoming one of the most notorious cony-catchers among the Inns-of-Court gallants, leading others like himself into ruin and degradation. The benchers at the Inns were well aware of the social temptations of the city and tried to keep the worst abuses under control, but disciplinary measures were not always strictly enforced and, thus, remained largely ineffective. It was undoubtedly for reasons such as these that the universities during the Caroline period replaced the Inns as the finishing schools for the landed gentry.[28]

In their evaluation of seventeenth-century legal education, modern legal historians strongly support the views expressed by contemporary satire, although recent emphasis has concentrated upon such matters as the relaxation of rules governing promotion, the introduction of mass callings to the bar, and the collapse of the readership system. It is doubtful whether any educational program could have survived the diversions and strife of pre-Commonwealth London. As A. W. B. Simpson remarks, "The Civil War plunged the educational system of the Inn[s] into a state of disorder from which it never recovered, and in the 1650s the beginning of the end was heralded by the development of a common practice of calling persons to the bar in return merely for a promise to buckle to and read. In spite of earnest efforts after the Restoration to preserve the old system by imposing fines for failure to read, it is plain that members of the Inn[s] preferred to pay such fines rather than devote their time to legal education."[29] Also, if one may judge from the continued popularity of legal texts, particularly the printing of books of quaeres and the famous readings, the student must have been forced to work more on his own, and with the help of tutors. Sir Matthew Hale reinforces this impression when he encourages students to follow his own method of compiling up-to-date abridgements based upon Brooke and Rolle.[30] Nevertheless, if the benchers themselves did not set an example, it could scarcely be expected of the students. One may receive a glimpse of Restoration discipline in hall when the "Lawyerus Bootatus et Spurratus" (1691) in open defiance of the benchers, joins his friend Fled-wit in a resolve "never to break our Brains with *Cook* upon *Littleton, Plowden, Keeble,* or *Fitzherbert*: No, let the Fraternity prate their Unintelligible Jargon at the Bar till their Lungs ake, we have found out a more pleasant way of Living."[31] Given the prior history of law satire, they were not establishing any precedents.

The decline of educational standards at the Inns resulted in a virtual eclipse of legal development generally, as study became a chore and promotion depended more upon social skills and favor. According to Sir Frederick Pollock, the whole of the legal enterprise suffered from a debilitating sterility and lack of inspiration for close to a century: "The last three-quarters of the eighteenth century were, broadly speaking, as barren in the development of purely legal doctrine as they were fertile in political invention and speculation. Between Coke, the last great lawyer of the Tudor age, and Hardwicke and Foster, the first of the Hanoverian, we mark a few commanding figures of men who have given us classical judgements or treatises." Otherwise, "It was a time of commonplace, indifferently learned, and not always upright judges, who were ill enough reported for the most part, but perhaps no worse than they deserved to be." This dismal story is largely the result of the decay of learning at the Inns of Court which, according to Holdsworth, had ceased to be educational institutions at the beginning of the eighteenth century. What education was offered there was "a mere form." If lawyers received any adequate training, they obtained it working in the offices of the more efficient attorneys like Chapman's or Salkeld's. Otherwise, the general state of legal education reached its nadir in the first decades of the eighteenth century. In Alan Harding's estimation, "the Inns of Court and Chancery were even more decayed than the eighteenth-century universities. New chambers were still being built, but Clements Inn was accommodating local brewers, periwig-makers, and comedians from Drury Lane, and demanding dues from members gone abroad and unheard of 'for above fifteen years past'. The inns were used as clubs by gentlemen of all sorts—politicians, and literary men like Aubrey and Evelyn—who continued to join them."[32]

The Inns of Chancery had also undergone their own process of decline and decay. At first devoted to the training of attorneys, in their heyday valued as "preparatory colleges for younger students" before admission to the Inns of Court, they had received a number of serious setbacks as early as 1557 and 1574 when, by order of the Privy Council, attorneys and solicitors were prohibited from membership at the Inns of Court.[33] It was felt that the reputation of the senior Inns was being seriously impaired by close association with the attorneys and solicitors. Most authorities, in fact, believed that the serjeants and barristers were not to be blamed for charges of vice and corruption aimed at the profession. When legislation was passed in 1607 to reform professional abuses, it was specifically aimed at the "Multitudes and Misdemeanors of Attornies and Solicitors-at-law," exonerating the "practice of just and honest serjeants and counsellors-at-law" who had been "greatly slandered." Again in 1614, the four Inns issued a joint order to sever their association with a "profession whose ranks were being filled with every sort of ignoramus and scoundrel,"[34] Consequently, during the seventeenth century, the Inns of Chancery lost all prestige and beneficial contact with the superior Inns, while the system of education provided became less and less applicable to the practical and technical needs of the working attorney who, in any case, preferred apprenticeship and training under senior attorneys. In the eighteenth century, then, education was virtually nonexistent at the Inns of Chancery, mirroring the plight of the senior Inns. As Robson points out, the "Inns of Chancery declined because the sort of education they could provide—occasional readings by some barrister from the Inns of Court which patronized them—was totally inadequate for the sort of work which the attorney was called upon to do."[35] To make matters worse, the apprentice program for attorneys and solicitors was also ineffectively administered, for there was absolutely no guarantee (outside the recognized firms) of the quality of training received, and there were no minimum examination standards, and very little judicial investigation of candidates. Parliament attempted to introduce legislation to regulate the training and registration of attorneys, but such measures as the Act of 1729 proved largely futile because there was no general will to execute the statutory provisions. Many practitioners had no legal training whatsoever, particularly in the provinces where it was more difficult to regulate the pettifoggers. Virtually anyone with sufficient gall could hang up a shingle, and contemporary records show that many unscrupulous individuals, such as actors, schoolmasters, petty tradesmen, and even clergymen, took advantage of the laxity of eighteenth-century judicial control of the legal profession.[36]

According to many commentators, the lion's share of legal education was informally conducted at taverns, private clubs, and coffeehouses rather than at the Inns. The diary of Sir Dudley Ryder, written during his student days, shows that precious little attention was paid to formal education at the Inns while considerable time was devoted to drinking, whoring, and playing pranks around town.[37] The future Chief Justice himself strongly disapproved of such pastimes and stoutly resisted the allurements of streetwalkers. John Baker, a civilized man who loved cricket, speaks of the "almost incredible habits of conviviality" which characterized the legal fraternity.[38] Accounts of the frivolous conduct of law students abound in eighteenth-century literature, and Ryder's confidences indicate that much of the professional satire is firmly grounded in the truth. He illustrates the type of law gossip which one might overhear in the lawyer's clubs, where aspiring students exercised their wits in arguing cases and outlining the most subtle ways of cheating clients. Ryder, a retiring soul, resolved to shun such fraudulent practices, and his accounts of these meetings actually inculpate the higher ranks of the profession.[39] The pages of contemporary journals contain numerous attacks upon the loose morality and rowdy behavior of law students. Even the mild-mannered Mr. Spectator complains of their lack of concern about legal studies and professional ethics, expressing a stern contempt for those young bloods who idle their mornings away at coffeehouses, affecting gallantry and fashionable deshabille. He also reports the activities of a group whose secret meetings he had managed to infiltrate, at which lawyers discussed various types of fraudulent practices which might be used against unsuspecting clients. He is appalled to learn that the greatest applause was accorded the individual who had achieved his deceitful objectives the most artfully.[40]

One of the severest critics of the coffeehouse lawyer is Henry Fielding, himself a lawyer and reared in a legal family.[41] His *Temple Beau* (1730) is perhaps the most extensive single treatment of the typical profligacy of the young lawyers at the Inns. In this early farce, the young Wilding has supposedly been studying law for six years at the Temple, all the while sending home staggering bills each quarter for the necessary books and supplies. He has actually been spending his money on elegant clothes, presents for his mistress, and visits to Paris. He knows absolutely nothing about the law, as he confesses to Bellaria, but his youthful escapades grind to a sudden halt when his father discovers the truth of the masquerade. His confession echoes the earlier satirical comments of Middleton, Jonson, and Ruggle: "You may as well think I am a scholar because I have been at Oxford as that I am a lawyer because I have been at the Temple."[42] Eight years later, two before he was called to the bar, Fielding was editing *The Champion*, which reveals the author's mature judgment of legal education. The comments of Hercules Vinegar, the Champion and self-elected judge of eighteenth-century morals, cut much deeper than the less informed satire of the stereotyped figure of Wilding in *The Temple Beau*:

> ...my Lord Coke, in his Comments on Littleton, insinuates that an academic education is the proper introduction to the study of laws.... Coke himself is (I am told) at present generally esteemed (especially by all those good judges who never read a syllable of him) to be a very stupid, dull fellow, who would have made a very indifferent figure in Westminster Hall in this age. I am assured by my son Tom Vinegar, who hath been a student in Lincoln's Inn these five years, that a very competent knowledge of the law is to be met in Jacob's Dictionary, and the other legal works of that learned author. Nay, he very confidently asserts, that nothing is more hurtful to a perfect knowledge of the Law than reading.... He confirms this with the example of some old plodders, who have lost themselves in the wood, without ever finding the road to business; and ludicrously says, the best advice to a student is not to outlaw himself.[43]

The spirit of Lawyerus Bootatus was alive and well, but fortunately there were still a number of serious plodders in the profession, maintaining the ancient traditions of scholarship—not the least of whom was the young Blackstone who also experienced some difficulty in "finding the way to business." Yet it was largely through the work of men like Blackstone, Viner, and Chambers that legal education was revolutionized at a crucial time in history.[44] The unfortunate aspect of Blackstone's career is that he undertook his work at a time when the law itself was about to undergo a century of rapid and extensive change; thus, because of his conservatism and because he was not a legal philosopher like Bentham, he has unfairly come to represent all that went before him.

Some years after Blackstone had "bid farewell to his muse," Robert Lloyd encouraged the young George Colman to make a similar decision.[45] The poem in which Lloyd discusses legal education is an excellent piece which provides insights into the consequences of such a career choice. Like his famous predecessor, Colman will discover that legal studies leave no time for the classics and that his favorite authors like Virgil and Pope will find little available space on bookshelves which will then groan "beneath th' unusual charge / Of Records, Statutes, and Reports at large." He warns that the temptations facing Colman are capable of distracting the indolent and less-gifted student. Because "the Depth of Law asks study, thought, and care," many throw up their hands in despair and waste their time and money in mindless diversions. The person who thinks he can varnish over his lack of ability only "nonsuits" himself and makes himself a figure of contempt. With trenchant irony, Lloyd scalps the wastrels and the beaux:

> What is to him dry cases, or dull report,
> Who studies fashions at the Inns of Court;
> And proves that thing of emptiness and show,
> That mungrel, half-form'd thing, a Temple Beau?
> Observe him sauntring up and down,
> In purple slippers, and in silken gown;
> Last night's debauch, his morning conversation;
> The coming, all his evening preparation.

Such gallants fail because they attempt the impossible: "to jumble wit and law together." Success in one will not induce success in the other, and least of all does the poet minimize the difficulties of the law, the dullness of reports, the arid hours of poring over cases. Colman's decision must take full account of the hardships:

> Knowledge in Law care only can attain,
> Where honour's purchas'd at the price of pain.
> If, Loit'ring, up th' ascent you cease to climb,
> No starts of labour can redeem the time.
> Industrious study wins by slow degrees,
> True sons of Coke can ne'er be sons of ease.

Despite these conservative notions of legal education, the poet senses and anticipates the need for extensive legal reforms. There is an air of optimism in Lloyd's eulogy of great lawyers, especially in the way he looks to Lord Mansfield to sweep the cobwebs out of the law and "to marry Common Law to Common Sense." Far less traditional than Blackstone, Lloyd momentarily follows Fielding's lead in deriding the old plodders of the law, who "tread the path their dull forefathers trod, / Doom'd thro' law's maze, without a clue, to range, / From second *Vernon* down to second *Strange*." The poet ridicules them, however, not because they study reports and plough through Coke but because they fail to understand the purpose of such exercises. The law *is* a maze to those benighted souls who remain unaware of practical needs. To a large extent, Lloyd's poem reflects the new moderation in mid eighteenth-century satire, reinforcing the impression gained by reading much greater writers like Fielding, Smollett, and Dr. Johnson. Few of these authors relaxed their vigil against corruption in law practice, but the criticism becomes much more measured and responsible. One notices a trend on the part of these satirists to represent the Temple beaux, the venal justices, and the corrupt lawyers as the exceptions to the respectable and praiseworthy rule exemplified in the careers of men like Foster, Hardwicke, Mansfield, Pratt, and Thurlow. The fact remains, however, that before 1750, the satirical representations of the common lawyer are often firmly anchored in historical realities as reflected in a wide range of popular sources.

3

Representations of Pettifoggery

> Let these
> Insnare the wretched in the toils of law,
> Fomenting discord, and perplexing right,
> An iron race!
>
> James Thomson, *The Seasons*

THE HISTORY OF PETTIFOGGING is much older than the term itself, which was probably coined at some time in the middle of the sixteenth century.[1] From the first, it was usually employed to describe the activities of those lawyers of inferior status who use mean, sharp, and caviling tactics in the conduct of petty litigation. Although occasionally used to describe other professionals, the word quickly specialized in its sole application to lawyers. In a broad sense, pettifogging and legal abuses are synonymous. The chief marks of the pettifogger are a lack of education, ambidextry (the crime of exacting fees from both parties to a lawsuit), overcharging on his bill of fees, self-enrichment to the ruin of the client, and deliberate contentiousness in stirring up civil disputes.[2] Similarly, no clear boundary exists between the character of the pettifogger and that of other *representative* lawyers, except as they combine certain satirical and critical conventions. The pettifogger, then, may frequently be characterized as a devil or diabolically inspired, as an ignoramus, or as lust-driven. Conversely, any of these satirical types may employ tactics which may be styled pettifoggery. However, this term provides a convenient rubric under which to discuss the more generalized conventions of law satire, and to mention those historical individuals who have brought dishonor and disrepute to the legal profession. In terms of higher law and professional ethics (if unwritten and rarely enforced), the pettifogger is ultimately not to be considered a lawyer at all. He *is* an intruder, an impostor, and a parasite of the law, whose customary fate is to be exposed, humiliated, or pitched over the bar. Even where he escapes the usual fate, he is the representation of all those behaviors which the law will not normally tolerate.

The Pettifogger and the Litigious Spirit

Near the conclusion of *James the Fourth,* Robert Greene introduces an intriguing choric scene in which a divine, a merchant, and a lawyer engage in an argument about the "manners and the fashions of this age." The debate is horizontally structured in the sense that no authority or higher power dominates the discussion or resolves the points at issue. In fact, each character offers a strong argument to support the views of his own profession. The lawyer's point that the corruptions of the age stem from

> A wresting power that makes a nose of wax
> Of grounded law, a damn'd and subtle drift
> In all estates to climb by other's loss,
> An eager thirst of wealth, forgetting truth

is never refuted although the divine contends that lawyers thrive upon civil strife and that "our state was first, before you grew so great, / A lantern to the world for unity."[3] The appeal to the ancient unity of mankind totally overlooks the lawyer's more pragmatic assessment of the problems confronting society: a shifting in the ancient social structure of the three estates, the general desire for improved social status, and the litigiousness of the citizenry. If lawyers are among the "patrons of our strife," they are merely implementing the public will, acting as agents of that wresting power that makes a mockery of grounded law. It is clear, though not expressly stated, that Greene's lawyer is a representative member of his profession and that he speaks on behalf of those lawyers who have not forgotten the principles of grounded law. The lawyers castigated by the divine are in fact those pettifoggers who seek only to profit from the greed and restlessness of the people, and the priest's criticism is generalized against the entire profession. The lawyer's analysis recognizes a distinction between the representation of the pettifogger and the representation of honest lawyers who in fact cherish ancient values.

Greene's lawyer is also typical of his profession in his pragmatic evaluation of the situation. He is concerned about grounded law, but he seems less interested in the remoter origins of civil strife. The divine is less than fair when he speaks as though the law invented the evils which maim the state. The wresting power deplored by Greene was nothing new in the late sixteenth century. If the late fifteenth century and early sixteenth century witnessed the evils of enclosure, rebellion, and the rise of monopolies, the Middle Ages provided enough evidence of an eager thirst of wealth just as turbulent and violent, much of which can be traced to ecclesiastical policies. The law did not invent these evils; it found them already flourishing, classified them, gave them names, and fought a continuing battle to bring them under control. That civil strife was frequently encouraged by lawyers goes without saying, but these are the lawyers who became the targets of literary satire, and of statutes.

The medieval preacher (like the Puritans later) seems more interested in attacking vice than extolling virtue, but he did not have an all-embracing term to describe abuses of the law. He classified most instances of wresting power under the heading of *avaritia*. Perhaps the closest terms for the types of abuses we usually associate with pettifoggery are "questmongering" and "maintenance," except that neither term need refer to the activities of men in law in particular. Powerful barons, landed gentry, rich merchants, and even divines often tampered with justice on their own behalf, while much of the lawlessness of the Middle Ages can be directly traced to dishonest officials such as sheriffs, bailiffs, coroners, and stewards. The author of the *Book of Vices and Virtues* describes the law as a mammoth conspiracy of the rich against the poor. The fifth branch of avarice is the "synne of bailyves, schereves, and seriauntes, that doth enditen and bryngeth in gret blame pore men to make hem geve hem or othere of here good, and dryveth hem to assyses and marchalsie for to wynne of hem wrongfully biside forth. And to false iustices longeth manye of these synnes, and to false questemongers, and to fals men of lawe, as pletours and advocates, as we have spoke to-fore."[4] Another anonymous preacher suggests that the law encourages litigious conduct and breeds perjury. Questmongering is the "raveyn of fals iures that goyn on qwestes and day holdynges, that for wynnynge of a litill worldely good, othur favour, or els of lordeshippe love or drede, puttis up fals enditementis, wronge evidence to qwestes in assyses to make trew men to lese ther good and ther lyvelode, or som tyme ther liffe, or els to flee ther countrey."[5] Chaucer's Parson, one of the two undeniably ideal figures among the pilgrims, also classifies questmongering with the sin of avarice and with the sin of bearing false witness against one's neighbor, either to take away his good name or to "bireven hym his catel or his heritage." (10: 794-96). In most of this moral literature, the lawyer is simply grouped with other individuals connected with the law in some way, all of whom, laymen and professionals alike, are charged with seeking social and political advancement or with deliberate self-enrichment at the expense of the victims. In *Piers Plowman,* the lawyers seek only monetary gain: "Lawe is so lordlich, and loth to maken ende, / Withoute presentis or panis heo plesith wel fewe" (A,3,148-49), and John Gower devotes virtually the whole of book 6 of *Vox Clamantis* to a sustained attack upon legal greed and the law's encouragement of litigation, its feeding upon the rich, and its oppression of the poor. Abuse of the law is possible because it is facilitated by all concerned in the process of litigation, from the false plaintiff to the bribable judge: "The first beth thilke that pleyneth falsely, that maketh and contriveth fals billes and fals suggestiouns and fals supplicaciouns or peticiouns, and sechen and pursuen false iugementes and longe delaies and fals wittenesses and fals pletours to meynteyne here false cause, and purchasen fals lettres of lordes bi fals suggestiouns for to greve and travaile men with wrong, or bi court of holi chirche, or bi lawe of the lond."[6] In other words, at the base of all medieval litigation, in spiritual and secular courts, is the law-mongering complainant. The moralists' accounts show that the courts would have had far less business without the litigiousness of greedy citizens. Bribes, perjury, forgery of letters and seals, and jury-tampering are only possible because of the public acceptance of these evils. Questmongering is an integral part of the pettifogger's world, so that it was inevitable that a class of dishonest lawyers would arise to undertake and prosecute false lawsuits given the presence of individuals prepared to win at all costs.[7]

During the early development of the common law, the pettifogger was in a much better position to take advantage of the legal system itself, and there were fewer avenues for the law to monitor professional ethics. The giving of gifts was standard practice and, in fact, a major source of the judges' income. As Alan Harding explains, "Such oiling of the machinery of justice was accepted as normal and inevitable in the Middle Ages and long after, and simply reflects the importance of the law and the judges in aristocratic society. Many of the cases of the reviling and rabbling of judges which occurred are likely to have been the products of particular political situations . . . rather than of a general 'disdain for the law.'"[8] The medieval litigant was nothing if not pragmatic; he oiled the machine because it was possible and advisable to do so. However, if Englishmen accepted gifts and bribes as a matter of fact, as part of an established system which few men dared to challenge, they did not accept this practice as morally normal. Far from it, justice was always a cherished ideal, not only to moralizing preachers but to all men of education and good sense.

During the early fifteenth century, questmongering and civil strife became a problem of great political magnitude, as constant baronial warfare and rebellion raged virtually uncontrolled throughout England.[9] The *Paston Letters* describe in great detail the petty squabbles and the land-grabbing tactics of the powerful landowners of fifteenth-century Norfolk. Where the law faltered in establishing its authority, disputants resorted to force, and where the law was hostile or unsympathetic to certain factions, armed gangs were employed to intimidate jurors, witnesses, counsel, and judges alike.[10] Contemporary literature abounds with vivid allusions to such lawlessness. The shepherds in the famous *Second Shepherds Play* of the Wakefield Master complain about the arrogance of retainers and liverymen, while Mind, Will, and Understanding in *Wisdom Who Is Christ* comment upon the evils of maintenance, describing it as a kind of protection-racketeering. The poet Hoccleve warns the young prince Henry of the dangers of widespread abuses of the law and suggests that such lawlessness will cause the overthrow of his kingdom. To some extent, unscrupulous lawyers and judges, as in *The Tale of Gamelyn*, contributed to these evils, but more often than not they probably acted under duress and in fear of their lives.[11] In spite of the many statutes directed against livery and maintenance, and in spite of the work of special commissions and the intervention of the King's Council, this kind of civil strife remained a source of alarm until the Tudor period.[12] Even during the reigns of Henry VII and Henry VIII, periodic outbreaks of feuding among the more powerful magnates indicate that the problem had not been fully resolved, even though the awesome power of the Court of Star Chamber minimized these threats to the internal security of the realm.[13]

In the late Tudor period, the law had succeeded largely in its efforts to bring private warfare under control, but it achieved this success at the expense of increasing litigation. The country gentlemen now took their warfare into the courts, not less belligerent than their ancestors, still seeking to expand their domains to the ruin of less fortunate neighbors. In fact, few aspiring Englishmen had not been involved in civil suits in Shakespeare's time.[14] A few no doubt were simply trying to hang on to what they possessed, but at the other end of the spectrum, there were always the promoters, monopolists, and land-hungry merchants to keep the courts busy. The pettifogger did not have to look far for business. There were plenty of clients like the contentious knight Sir Mordicus in Sir John Davies's *The Scourge of Folly*, who

> is never out of Lawe,
> Since he had ought to goe to law withall;
> Hee'le trye an action with you for a straw,
> Nay for a looke, and much more for the wall:
> Yet though he thus be still in law and hate,
> An out-law is lesse hurtfull to the State.[15]

Davies of Hereford, a poet of some skill and reputation, was also a prominent serjeant-at-law and would, therefore, have a close familiarity with the social problems arising from the extreme litigiousness of the English knighthood. As a recent computerized study clearly shows, the landed gentry ranked high among the lawmongers of Elizabethan-Jacobean society, for Star Chamber records indicate that litigants were quite prepared to take whatever advantages they could over their opponents.[16] According to Michael Birks, "The Englishman's renewed respect for the processes of the law was not accompanied by any pressing sense of justice in his conduct of lawsuits. Court records show that he was prepared to use every trick imaginable to defeat his adversary. Forged writs, perjured evidence, and bribed juries were commonplace aids to the winning of actions. Conversely, lawsuits were often begun for no other purpose than to embarrass an enemy by making him incur legal costs—and the cost of litigation was then very much greater than it is today. Unfortunately for the legal profession the blame for all these malpractices attached itself to the lawyers rather than their employers. Even so a great deal of the opprobrium bestowed upon the profession was obviously well deserved."[17]

The emphasis Birks places upon the crucial role played by the greedy and unscrupulous litigant is amply reflected in the literature of the Tudor-Stuart periods. Stage lawyers are often accompanied by flocks of suitors, tripping and tumbling over each other in their desperate quest for clarification and assurance, and invariably fobbed off with curt, ambiguous answers, or ludicrously mollified by legal jargon.[18] La Writt (*The Little French Lawyer*), Bartolus (*The Spanish Curate*), and Griffin (*The Honest Lawyer*) are typically pursued by ignorant and greedy suitors. Middleton's Tangle (*The Phoenix*) has twenty-nine lawsuits running concurrently. Such characters exemplify the spirit of contention which threatens the peace and harmony of state and family. It is this same baleful influence which underlies much of the irresponsible criticism of the law itself, for, as Sir Matthew Hale shrewdly observes, "There is in mankind a passionate self-law, which makes men think that whatsoever crosseth them in their interest is unjust, and fit to be altered."[19] In its worst form, this self-law, another version of Greene's wresting power, compels the vicious individual to take the law into his own hands. An interesting real-life example of this kind of lawlessness, reported by Chamberlain, is the remarkable case of the murder of Sir John Tyndall, a Master of Chancery, in 1616. The assailant was an aged gentlemen by the name of Bartram who showed no sign of remorse when he was apprehended, believing that he had performed a service for the Commonwealth. According to Chamberlain, Bartram had declared that he had mistaken his mark, "and should rather have shot hail shot at the whole Court, which indeed grows great and engrosses all manner of cases, and breeds generally complaint for a decree passed there this term (subscribed by all the King's learned Council) whereby that Court may review and call in question what judgments soever pass at Common Law; whereby the jurisdiction of that Court is enlarged out of measure, and so suits become as it were immortal."[20] One doubts whether Bartram actually thought of himself as an avenger dedicated to the reestablishment of the jurisdictional balance between Chancery and the Common Law courts. It also appears unusual for a commentator as customarily sensible as Chamberlain to report this crime in a manner justifying its commission. The sensational murder was later moralized in an anonymous pamphlet, in which the author attributes the so-called "resolution" of the old man to the Devil's inspiration. The author is outraged that so many persons actually sympathize with the murderer's age and misery. He points out that Bartram was an individual who had devoted many years to lawmongering, and his initial successes at law "made him more covetous in prosecuting such contentions."[21] When, however, the law ceased to run in his favor, the murderer, "being of a haughtie, turbulent, and disdainful spirit, full of rage, furie, and headlong indignation; propounding to himself that Sir *Iohn Tindall* was the onelie Calthrope throwne under his feete, to pricke him and cast him downe: Sealed a damnable vow betwixt hell and his soule to be revenged" (B1r) upon the Chancery Master whose report had ruined his estate. In other words, Bartram's case ought to serve as a lesson to those who lay the hand of oppression upon the poor, for Bartram is chiefly to blame because he had ruined himself by thirty years and more of lawmongering. As John Clapham, secretary of the Court of Wards, remarks, "So much more is it safe for a man to sit down with a certain loss of a part of his estate, being questionable by law, than with disquiet mind, waste of time, expense of money, long and unfruitful attendance, to make shipwreck of the whole, as many men, abused by mis-informations, or transported with wilful malice, have oftimes done."[22] The lawyer-poet George Gascoigne offers the same advice in his *Dulce Bellum Inexpertis*:

> If common people could foresee the fine
> Which lights at last by lashing out at lawe,
> Then who best loves this question, *Myne or Thyne,*
> Would never grease the greedy serjeants pawe,
> But sit at home and learne this old sayde sawe,
> *Had I revenged bene of every harme,*
> *My coate had never kept me halfe so warme.*[23]

Knowing full well the unpredictability of lawsuits, perceptive lawyers have rarely gone to law for themselves.

In Bernard's *The Isle of Man,* an allegory based upon legal proceedings, the willfull and malicious prosecution of suits is associated with the activities of Covetousness, who has wielded an inordinate influence over the civil government of Manshire for many years. When the arch-malefactor is arraigned before the idealized Justice, the prosecutor Commonwealth demonstrates by a skillful use of witnesses the falsity of Covetousness's claim to the name of Thrift and proves that "hee (as your Lordship well knoweth) hath miserably corrupted the course of Iustice, by briberie, by making many Lawyers pleade for more Fees, than honestly, for the equalitie of the cause; by delaying the cause, by removing it from one Court to another, till men bee undone." He has succeeded in his abuse of the law by appealing to the litigiousness of the less principled citizens and by all the means normally employed by corrupt lawyers: "He hath, to get his desire, suborned false witnesses, counterfeited Evidences, and forged Wils."[24] Only in the ideal worlds, such as Arcadia, Utopia, and Manshire, do pettifogging lawyers totally fail. In the real world, malpractice flourishes because litigants make it possible by their eager acceptance of corrupt practices. In large measure, the legal world of Elizabethan and Jacobean society was the creation of the client, and, as W. J. Jones remarks, "It was useless to try to restrain litigation by making lawyers aware of their presumed responsibilities. The gentlemen of England intended to call the tune when it came to mapping out the broad outlines of a litigious campaign. And so, despite the usual hostility towards lawyers, there was an increasing demand for their services, and there might still be something in the old rumour that a man's local prestige was enhanced by the number of lawyers on his payroll."[25]

Because he is the agent of the litigious client, the pettifogging lawyer is a personification of the client's greed. His aim is to profit from the avarice of others and to fatten himself on their malice, yet greed and malice are the pettifogger's own besetting sins. When Lincus is exiled from Arcadia, he does not despair, for he anticipates success in the outside world:

> For I have all those helpes my skill requires,
> A wrangling nature, a contesting grace,
> A clamorous voyce, and an audacious face.
> And I can cite the law t'oppugne the law,
> And make the glosse to overthrow the text;
> I can alledge and vouch authority,
> T'imbroyle th'intent, and sense of equity;
> Besides, by having beene a Notary,
> And us'd to frame litigious instruments
> And leave advantages for subtility
> And strife to worke on, I can so devise
> That there shall be no writing made so sure
> But it shall yeeld occasion to contest
> At any time when men shall thinke it best.
> (lines 2924-37)

In Arcadia he fails because there are no writings to be misconstrued, nor men who think it best to contest what they hold in common. Lincus is typified throughout as a charlatan, and his remarks about his training as a notary indicate that he is not qualified to be a lawyer.

In many works, the pettifogger is similarly represented as an outright impostor. Throte, the rascally attorney of Barrey's *Ram-Alley*, has only sufficient cunning to deceive the uneducated and foolish denizens of the London underworld. The perceptive characters immediately detect his fraudulent tactics. Small-shanke describes him as

> one that professeth law, but indeed
> Has neither law nor conscience, a fellow

That never saw the barre, but when his life
Was cald in question for a coosenage.
(A4r)

And when Mistress Taffeta and Adriana discuss marital expectations, the latter rejects the suggestion of Throte's suitability, not because he is a lawyer but indeed because he is not. She says that Throte has never seen the inside of an Inn of Court and has probably only served in a menial capacity at some Inn of Chancery. When Throte has the effrontery to propose marriage to Justice Tuchin's niece, the old attorney is soundly rebuked:

You sir *Ambo-dexter,*
A Sumners sonne and learnt in *Norfolk* wiles,
Some common baile, or Counter Lawyer,
Marry my neece?
(G4v)

He is sent off to the Fleet prison at the Justice's order, where he is bested in a mock-trial by Wil Small-shanke in a flurry of law terms. Middleton's Tangle passes himself off as a solicitor, but he is actually a seasoned litigant who knows more than most attorneys. He earns money to support his own litigation by giving advice to other clients.

The pettifogger's success depends entirely upon his ability to stir up civil strife, and his skill at "setting people by the ears together" becomes the most constant feature of his typical representation, a convention grounded in historical reality. As the Elizabethan topographer William Harrison observes, the pettifogger often employs brokers "to kindle and espy coals of contention whereby the one side may reap commodity and the other spend and be put to travail," and he provides a number of examples in various counties of men who had reaped huge profits by such tactics.[26] The moralist Philip Stubbes cites the biblical text "vengeance is mine, and I wil reward" and blames the law for its failure to appease and arbitrate controversies, but although he castigates lawyers who make a profit out of civil strife, he places the chief blame upon the litigants. In response to Theodorus's surprise that the people are "quarrelous," Amphilogus remarks that they "are very contentious indeed. Insomuch as, if one give never so small occasion to another, sute must straight be commenced; and to lawe they go, as round as a ball, till either both, at least the one, become a beggar all daies of his life after."[27] Only the lawyer who spurs the contention forward inevitably wins; all else is left to blind chance.

Barnabe Rych, while confessing that his "skill is unable to render due reverence to the honourable Iudges" and "the honest reputation of a number of learned lawyers," laments the loss of good faith caused by those lawyers "that do multiply suites, and draw on quarrels betweene friend and friend, betweene brother and brother, and sometimes between the father and the sonne... that can make good shift to send their clients home with penniles purses...."[28] He observes that some lawyers complain about the lack of business and say that "men are become to be more wise in these days, then they have beene in former ages, and rather put uppe a wrong than fee a Lawyer"; but he says, "I do not thinke there is any such wisedome in this age, when there are so many wrangling spirits, that they are so ready to commence suites, but for a neighbours goose, that shall but happen to looke over a hedge," and he likens the situation to an occasion when too many guests arrive at a party and fight about the lack of chairs. In other words, there were too many lawyers rather than insufficient business, and by far the largest contingent within the profession are "these Atturnies, Soliciters, and such other petty *Foggers,* where there be such abundance, that the one of them can very hardly thrive by the other; And this multitude of them do trouble all the parts of England" (B4v).

The overpopulation of the profession was a commonplace of Tudor-Jacobean satire, but recent research has revealed that there was not an overwhelming increase in the numbers of barristers called to the bar, and thus the problem stems from the steady rise in the numbers of attorneys registered at Westminster Hall. Furthermore, there must have been many individuals who were masquerading as attorneys who were neither qualified nor officially recognized.[29]

For the highly experienced and well qualified attorneys and barristers there was always sufficient litigation to keep them profitably and honorably occupied. If anything, the successful lawyers were too successful, so that younger lawyers, who failed to establish an immediate reputation and who did not gain favor, were often condemned to penury and oblivion. If there were dishonest men practicing at the bar, they probably came from this lower stratum of individuals who had to scrape a living from the law as best they could. Doubtless, some of these less successful lawyers were forced occasionally to compromise their sense of integrity by taking cases from the pettifoggers. Allowing this assumption, we can see that the less scrupulous and the least qualified, according to contemporary accounts, were compelled to breed contention in order to survive. Sir Thomas Wilson's *The State of England* (1600) attributes much of the turmoil to this kind of malpractice:

> And since the longe continuance of peace hath bred an inward canker and unrest in menn's myndes, the people doeing nothinge but iarre and wrangle one with another, thes lawyers by the ruines of neighbours contencions ar growne so great, so rich and so proud, that no other sort dare medle with them; their number is so great now that... they can scarcely live on by an other, the practise being drawne into a few hand of those which are most renowned, and the rest live by pettifogging, seeking meanes to sett their neighbours att variance whereby they may gayne on both sides. This is one of the greatest inconveniences in the land, that the number of lawyers are

so great they undoe the country people and buy up all the lands that are to be sold, soe that yong gentlemen or others newly cominge to their livinges, some of them pryinge into his evidence will find meanes to sett him at variance with some other, or some other with him, by some pretence or quiddity, and when they have halfe consumed themselves in sute they are fayne to sell theyr land to follow the process and pay theire debts, and then that becomes a prey to laweyers.[30]

As a civil lawyer with a university education, Wilson may here be demonstrating his concern for the decline of prestige in the civil law degree, but we cannot dismiss his comments simply on these terms.[31] The tract reflects a concern for England's political stability which he presents as threatened by the rapid decay in moral and religious standards evidenced within the realm. In this larger context, Wilson's view of legal corruption and pettifoggery would not have been considered anomalous among his contemporaries, certainly not among the common lawyers. Davies of Hereford places human law within its orthodox religious and moral context in his *Microcosmos,* according to which the lawyer has a moral duty to *live,* not merely to practice, by the ancient maxims of Justice and Truth:

> For *Lawyers* ought (like *Lawes*) to make *Men*
> good,
> And who are in the *wronge,* or *Right,* reveale:
> Then are they worthy of al *livelyhood,*
> That makes men live in perfect *Brotherhood.*

Unfortunately, as Davies in his practical and professional wisdom knew full well, only the rare and most unusual lawyers achieve this kind of regard for social harmony. The temptations are too great, the attraction of wealth and prestige too powerful, so that even virtuous men have failed in their sacred task. Davies reserves his greatest contempt for those lawyers who exact the "treble fee" and who dwell in the "Babell-Towres of Pompe and Pride":

> ...a Petti-fogging prating *patch,*
> That gropes the *Law* for nothing but for *Galles,*
> Should be so prowde as if he had no match,
> For tossing *Lawes* as they were Tennis-*Bals,*
> This vexeth *God* and *Good-men* at the Galles:
> Yet such there are, (too many such there are,)
> Who are the *Seedes-men* of Litigious *Bralls:*
> And are so prowde that by the *Lawes* they dare
> Contend with *Crassus,* though they nought can spare.
> I graunt the *Law* to bee an holy *thing,*
> Worthy of *reverence* and all *regard,*

But the abuse of *Law* (and so of *King*)
By such as will abuse both for *reward,*
Is damn'd.[32]

Davies continues by wishing that all such lawyers could be disbarred, or even put
behind bars, yet he acknowledges the difficulty of taking action because too many
lawyers are patronized in their chicanery by the rich and powerful.

The point of many criticisms of the law during this period is not simply that
there are too many lawyers; that is only one-half of the satirical message. For
most commentators like Davies, there are rather too many "*Seedes-men* of
Litigious *Bralls.*" This distinction between honorable lawyers and their rabble-
rousing imitators is particularly noticeable in works dealing with law in terms of
cosmological associations such as Tisdale's *The Lawyer's Philosophy* (1622), in
which true lawyers bask in the light of wisdom and pettifoggers are mere
shadowy "*fire-drakes,*" having no eternal substance or being.[33] In his "Democritus to the Reader," Robert Burton singles out pettifoggery as one of the chief
causes of civil disorder in England and equates litigious conduct with madness, a
disease which renders all men "giddy, vertiginous and lunatic within this
sublunary maze." So many lawsuits, contentious lawyers, and confusing laws are
the inevitable symptoms of a distempered and melancholic nation:

> for where such kind of men swarm, they will make more work for themselves, and
> that body politic diseased, which was otherwise sound. A general mischief in these
> our times, an insensible plague, and never so many of them … and for the most part
> supercilious, bad, covetous, litigious generation of men … a clamorous company,
> gowned vultures … thieves and seminaries of discord; worse than any pollers by the
> highway side … that take upon them to make peace, but indeed are the very
> disturbers of our peace, a company of irreligious harpies, scraping, griping
> catchpoles (I mean our common hungry pettifoggers, *rabulae forensis,* love and
> honour in the meantime to all good laws, and worthy lawyers, that are so many
> oracles and pilots of a well-governed common-wealth), without arts, without
> judgment.[34]

Burton's frequent use of medical images is part of his larger plan of dissecting the
commonwealth as a metaphorical body, and in this context, the work of the
pettifogger must be viewed as if he represents an excessive influx of the
melancholic humor (black bile) into the nation's system. The soul of the state can
only be restored to harmony by rebalancing the peccant humors, but this
equilibrium will be difficult to effect in times when melancholia and choler
(yellow bile) rage out of control. The disturbances created by wrangling lawyers
are the natural outcome of these excessive humors, where melancholia is equated
to cunning and treachery, choler to wrath and spite. In describing the typical
conduct of these *rabulae forensis* (court rabble), Burton demonstrates how craft
combines with the wrangling spirit to proliferate civil disputes: "If there be no

jar, they can make a jar, out of the law itself find still some quirk or other, to set them at odds, and continue causes so long, *lustra aliquot* [for decades], I know not how many years before the cause is heard, when 'tis judged and determined, by reason of some tricks and errors it is as fresh to begin, after twice seven years sometimes, as it was at first; and so they prolong time, delay suits, till they have enriched themselves and beggared their clients."[35] It is also necessary to underline the distinction Burton makes between the pettifogger and the honest lawyers whose practice actually undergirds the well-governed commonwealth.

Davies's reference to the proverbial role of Crassus introduces yet another constant theme, the relationship between legal abuses and the deadly sins. According to authorities like Davies, Burton, and Tisdale, it is pride and avarice which motivate the pettifogger. His career is dedicated to self-aggrandizement and the acquisition of money and power. Dekker's *Seven Deadly Sins of London* demonstrates that the sins have conspired to overthrow the peace and harmony of the city, and each contingent of sins has its company of lawyers.[36] Another contemporary tract, *The Returne of the Knight of the Poste From Hell* (1606), clearly associates the work of pettifoggers with the deadly sin of pride:

> Now to conclude, that Pride may be compleate in all his proceedinges: there is sent into the worlde certaine Furies of Hell, who in the habites of Petty-foggers, or unlawful Lawyers, runne aboute to disturbe Peace, and overthrow friendship, to breake the bonde of nature, and the chaine of allegance, by ringing in mens eares, the properties of mine and thine, the bewty of commandement, and the glory of large possessions, that it is fit eyther to be none, or else alone. That to imitate Princes, is to be without Competitors, and it springes that Envie being an Assistant with Avarice sets all the world together, by the eares. These Ministers of the infernall Kingdome, abusing Law, and misconstruing the iudgements of most learned Sages, with the base corruptions of their muddie consciences, these are they which have double tongs, and two folde solutions, one for private discourse, and another for publike profite....[37]

The anonymous moralist offers no analysis of law and assumes that the reader is aware of the truth which illuminates "the iudgements of most learned Sages." His chief concern is to show the total effect of the workings of the sins, to demonstrate their interdependence and mutual reinforcement. The infernally inspired lawyers must also be judged as conspirators against peace, but their success depends upon the cooperation of all elements within society. The combined assault of politicians, corrupt officials, lawyers, merchants, usurers, and physicians is directed at the very heart of traditional order, and, if successful, will produce the kind of chaos feared by men like Barnabe Rych, of friend against friend, brother against brother, father against son, subject against ruler, and ultimately of man against God. In this, the pettifogger plays a central and symbolic role.

The characters produced by writers like Overbury, Earle, Stephens, and Butler furnish an interesting synopsis of seventeenth-century criticism of these non-lawyers. Overbury's title "A Meere Common Lawyer" puns on the phrase "common law," but the figure stigmatized by the author is really not a lawyer at all, although common enough. He is a man of more substance among "his Countrie Neighbours," but they, "poore soules, take Law and Conscience, Court and Chancery for all one." The pettifogger makes a name for himself because of his rustic skill "from putting Riddles and imitating *Merlines* Prophesies" and his experience in setting all "together by the eares." Overbury does not satirize the legal profession generally, although he states that "many of the same coate, which are much to be honor'd, partake of divers of his indifferent qualities," but he warns that it is necessary not to mistake the mark. The *"Discretion, Virtue,* and sometimes other good *learning,* concurring for distinguishing ornaments to them make him as a foile, to set their worth on."[38] This portrait is expanded in Webster's "A Meere Petifogger," which emphasizes the spirit of contention to a greater degree than Overbury's character. Filled with guile and treachery, the pettifogger is "one of *Sampsons Foxes*: He sets men together by the eares, some more shamefully than *Pillories*; and in a long Vacation his sport is to goe Fishing *with the Penall Statutes*," for he is "an Earthquake that will willingly let no ground lie in quiet."[39] Earle's "Atturney" talks like a lawyer and fosters the air of an individual who "had mooted seven yeeres in the Inns of Court when all his skil is stucke in his girdle, or in his office window." He is highly regarded by the village churls, and he has made a fortune stirring up strife.[40] Stephens's "A Meere Atturney" is "fit for all turnes that any way enrich his Cofer: for he hath knavery enough to cosen the people, but wit enough to deceive the gallowes." Likewise, he is a great agitator who has made "sub-paenas, Executions, and all Writs of quarrell be his bondslaves."[41] Even fifty years later, Samuel Butler's portrait of a pettifogger includes the same representational features:

> He is a Kind of Law-Hector, that lives by making Quarrels between Man and Man, and prosecuting or compounding them to his own Advantage. He is a constant Frequenter of country Fairs and Markets, where he keeps the Clowns in Awe with his Tricks in Law, and they fear him like a Conjurer or a cunning Man. He is no Gentleman, but a Varlet of the Long-robe, a Purveyor of Suits and Differences, most of which he converts to his own Benefit, and the rest to the Use of those he belongs to. He is a Law-seminary, that sows Tares amongst Friends to entangle them in Contention with one another, and suck the Nourishment from both. He is like a Ferret in a Coney-Borough, that drives the poor silly Animals into the Purse-Net of the Law, to have their skins stripped off, and be preyed upon.[42]

Uniformly, in all these representations, the pettifogger is the predator, who achieves his end by stirring up trouble among the ignorant and gullible. He always achieves his greatest triumphs in the country where he experiences little difficulty in intimidating the rustics. When the satirist wishes to delineate the features of the honest lawyer, he normally reverses the conventional details of the pettifogger's representation. Thus, unlike his wrangling counterpart, the honest lawyer delights "to be an Arbitrator, not an Incendiary... and advises people to compose their *assaults* and *slanders* over the same *Ale* that *begot* them... and the old Emblem of the *Brambles* tearing oft the *sheeps* fleece that ran to it for *shelter* in a *storm,* can have no reflection upon him, whose *Brain* is as active, and his *Tongue as voluble* for a penniless Pauper, as when *Oyl'd* with the *aurum potabile* of a *Dozen Guinnies.*"[43] One could almost believe that this portrait was written with the texts of Overbury, Earle, Gardyne, Stephens, and Butler by the author's side; for, however defensive and apologetic this positive character sketch may appear, it amply reinforces the representational pattern: namely the pettifogger is all that the true lawyer is not.

During the Commonwealth, the same charges are repeated in the many attacks upon the legal profession, although the satirical tone darkens into pure invective. We hear less about honest members of the profession, and the defeated client is more often treated as the victim of political treachery than of his own litigiousness and gullibility. Virtually all lawyers are pettifoggers. The anonymous pamphleteer of *A Looking-Glasse for All Proud, Ambitious, Covetous, and Corrupt Lawyers* allows no exceptions. Affluence has corrupted the ancient streams of the law, and from the beginning, the common lawyer has been motivated by greed and political influence: "When abundant wealth brought in luxurie to afflict the manners of the Common-Wealth, they grew into corruption with the times, tooke fees, and became *viles rabulae,* Hackney Pettyfoggers, and Hucksters of the Law." The law has been betrayed from within, and their combined wisdom has not been able to cure the foul ulcer of "all our legall grievances." "These Sonnes of the Law have turned justice into wormwood: the honourable profession of the Law *in artem litigandi,* into the trade of brabbling and pettifogging. It were a worke of infinite labour to trace halfe their misdemeanours. They are

> *Turba gravis paci, placidaeque inimica quieti,*
> *Quae semper miseras sollicitabit opes.*
> Foes to sweet peace, and unto pleasing rest,
> Which miserable wealth do still molest."[44]

Even after the Civil War, when the Rump parliament had introduced certain reforms, the radicals continued to press for the redress of further grievances. The voluble Mercurius Rhadamanthus devotes an issue of *The Chiefe Iudge of Hell* to each of the central courts, with two for the Upper Bench (one to the civil side and one to the criminal side of the court). In each pamphlet, he comes to an identical conclusion: that the sole aim of the courts is self-enrichment and self-perpetuation. Justice is entirely irrelevant to the *being* of these courts, for each is organized mainly to benefit its own burgeoning staff of clerks, prothonotaries, attorneys, six-clerks, examiners, and solicitors. To pay this army of lawyers, the courts systematically fleece the people by charging innumerable and exorbitant fees.[45] The authorities were painfully aware of this problem and made a number of attempts to establish a reasonable calendar of fees, but given the strict surveillance of the court officials against such intrusions upon their domains, most attempts at reform were either short-lived or totally fruitless. Even Cromwell and his army could make little impression upon the Court of Chancery whose officials continually ignored the protector's ordinances.[46]

The pure radicals, of course, desired less to reform particular abuses than to abolish the legal profession altogether. Mercurius Democritus exulted in the hope that the army would send the lawyers packing, "furnished with forks and rakes against the next hay-time," and he writes the following piece of doggerel to celebrate the prospect:

> The honest soldier welcome is to town
> That puts the lawless rooking lawyer down
> His fees must be far lower rated
> His writs must now be new translated
> Corruption banished quite out of town
> Justice shall put all knavery down.[47]

Also, sundry "well-affected" citizens of London expressed the hope that parliament would see fit to reduce the lawyers "to a sad condition," a work they recommended as "well pleasing to the Lord." In spite of the glorious victories of the army and the sweeping reforms introduced by parliament, they still did not feel safe with lawyers on the prowl:

> For if there be a generation of men yet remaining amongst us that turn judgment into gall and the fruit of righteousness into hemlock, that oppress the widow and the fatherless and turn aside the stranger from his right, that feed upon afflicted prisoners and nourish the cruelty of jailers, *lawyers are the men.*[48]

Even if one admits that the above-cited passages represent the most extreme instances of root-and-branch criticism of the law, the spirit typified by such reckless and impractical proposals nevertheless comprises a large proportion of the anti-law writings of the interregnum. The few pieces in defense of the legal profession came chiefly from the pens of lawyers, and even the more measured comments of the Puritan moderates all too often sway in the direction of extremist viewpoints. In such a climate, then, it was small wonder that enlightened men like Hale, Rolle, Widdrington, and Whitelocke were slow to act. Hale surely had many of these radical pamphleteers in mind when he attributed the reforming zest of the previous age to "passionate self-law."[49] It is self-law, of course, that makes law indispensable.

After the Restoration, the pettifogger remains a stock figure, with little change in the representation of his character, and the same old charges are leveled against the profession. As Barbara Shapiro observes, "If the judges eventually gained a reputation for honesty and impartiality, the same could not be said of lawyers, court officials, and clerks. Lawyers, particularly attorneys and solicitors, were attacked for promoting and unnecessarily prolonging lawsuits, greed, confusing laymen, and demonstrating inadequate training"; however, six bills considered by parliament between 1666 and 1709 yielded no legislation regulating the numbers or the abuses of attorneys. Shapiro's findings are further confirmed by the contemporary authority of Sir Matthew Hale in his *History of the Common Law of England,* in which the author lists a number of needed reforms, including a reduction in the "multitudes of Attorneys practising in the Great Courts at Westminster, who are ready at every Market to gratify the Spleen, Spite or Pride, of every Plaintiff."[50]

In order to recognize the longevity of satirical representations of the pettifogger, it is necessary to compare the features of the characters written in the seventeenth century with those produced at the beginning of the eighteenth. In most of these later portraits, we find the greatest emphasis still placed upon the pettifogger's ability to foment civil discord. James Puckle tells a story about a typical wrangling attorney, "a Nitt of the law, who made it as much his care and business to create feuds, and animate difference, as the Vestal virgins us'd to maintain the sacred fire," who when he was in his cups, "boasted himself an attorney, And That he had a knack of improving trifles, and frivolous contests, into good fat causes, as he call'd 'em. That he could set man and wife at variance the first day of their marriage, and parents and children the last moments of their lives." Puckle uses the comments of his attorney to moralize on the stupidity of going to law and retells Boileau's celebrated tale of the travelers who, quarreling about the possession of an oyster, submit their difference to a lawyer. Having heard the matter in dispute, the lawyer "whipp'd out his knife, open'd the oyster, swallow'd the fish, gave the plaintiff and defendant each a shell, and gravely went his way." Such stories were popular during the eighteenth century. Pope and Prior both wrote versions of the oyster case, and Puckle adds a story about a frog and a mouse who leave their dispute to the arbitration of a kite. Goldsmith's Citizen of the World tells a story of a grasshopper, whangam, serpent, yellow-bird, hawk, and a vulture, which ends predictably with the vulture gobbling up "the hawk, grasshopper, whangam, and all in a moment." The moral of all these stories is simply that the law is a devourer of those who stray into its clutches.[51]

Ned Ward includes a long portrait of a pettifogger in the Westminster Hall scene of *The London Spy,* in which all the commonest features of the typical representation receive the fullest elaboration. As may be expected, the most prominent identifying mark of his character is his dedication to civil disputes:

He's an amphibious monster, partaking of two natures, and those contrary; he's a great lover of peace and enmity and has no sooner set people together by the ears, but is soliciting the Law to make an end of the difference. His mother was a scold, and he was begot in a time when his father us'd the act more for quietness' sake than procreation. His learning is commonly as little as his honesty, and his conscience much larger than his green bag. His affection for the Law proceeds from the litigiousness of his ancestors, who brought the family to beggary.[52]

In spite of much boasting to the contrary, the pettifogger belongs to the very dregs of his profession, those who cannot lay fair claim to the title of lawyer, for his knowledge consists only of ploys and tricks to set the law against itself. Yet the most interesting feature of his portrait is the manner in which the pettifogger becomes, as it were, the spawn of the litigious client.[53] Also, in his mock epic, *A Journey to Hell* (1700), Ward amplifies his portrait of the pettifoggers as "a spurious sort" and "meer Locusts of the Court." Most of the pettifoggers, according to Ward, were never trained in the law but attached themselves like parasites to the courts:

> Some by their Shop-board Looks were Taylors bred,
> But broke, and on their Backs had scarce a Shred;
> Not only in their Lives, but Looks were Knaves,
> Litigious from their Cradles to their Graves.
> Vers'd in those Querks, amongst the Scribes they saw,
> After long Troubles did themselves withdraw,
> From making Sutes of Cloaths, to manage Suits of Law:
> Well knowing it requires an equal Skill,
> To make a Lawyers, or a Taylors Bill.
> Amongst this paltry Crew, were Ten to One
> Bred up to Trades, but by the Law undone:
> And thus distress'd, most equitably sought
> Relief from that which had their Ruin brought:
> Or else resolv'd, from being basely us'd,
> T'abuse the Law, by which they'd been abus'd.[54]

Although in this poem, and elsewhere, Ward attacks abuses perpetrated by the senior ranks of the profession, there is little doubt in his view that the worst failure of the law is its inability to control and regulate the activities of these pettifoggers.

Eighteenth-century satire also stresses the social danger of unabated pettifoggery. Just as Burton had considered the abuse of law a destroyer of political and social stability, later commentators like Thomas D'Urfey, Ned Ward, and Jonathan Swift warn that continuing civil disorder is a clear sign that lawful government could easily be swept away in a reign of tyranny. In his *Progress of Honesty*, D'Urfey associates litigious conduct and pettifoggery with the spirit of Discord and Treason, the two great enemies who have vowed the destruction of the kingdom. Dwelling "deep in a hollow, dark and dreadful Cave," they hatch their plots against Honesty and Resolution. While Treason resorts to violence, the design of weapons, and the spread of his poison, Discord relies upon plausibility and subtlety:

> *Discord's* Apartment different was seen,
>   He had a Lawyer been;
> One that if Fees were large could loudly bawl,
>   But had a Cough o'th' Lungs if small;
> And never car'd who lost so he might win:
> His shelves were cramm'd with Processes and Writs,
>   That dull'd poor Clients wits;
> Long Rolls of Parchment, Bonds, Citations, Wills,
> Fines, Executions, Errors, and eternal Chancery Bills:
>   This blessed Pair thought this obscure Retreat
> A Place most for their Purpose fit
> To forge their Villanies, and exclaim
> On Resolution's Name.[55]

Discord proceeds in his design by finding flaws in his adversary's title and by discrediting his reputation. The author does not carry out the full plot in these legal terms and perhaps does not need to. Having identified his arch-enemy as a lawyer, who marshals to his aid his formidable list of legal technicalities, D'Urfey doubtless feels that he has depicted an adversary greatly to be feared by the ignorant and politically unskilled.

To men of integrity and education, the wrangling lawyer is only an object of amusement and contempt, as Swift suggests.[56] Nonetheless, since they are often successful, the amusement is dearly purchased, and the contempt must be shared by those who either condone or ignore abuses of the law. The coalition between pettifogging law and ignorance is the central theme of Fielding's allegorical comedy *Pasquin* (1736).[57] In this play, the realm of Queen Common-Sense is invaded by the armies of the pretender Queen Ignorance. At the outset, we discover that the danger of usurpation is real, for Common-Sense has offended her chief counselors, Law, Physic, and Firebrand (Religion), and they are conspiring to throw their support to the invading Ignorance. Law is particularly upset because Common-Sense has stipulated that laws be written in the common language, and when the queen questions him about various abuses, he insolently replies, "Madam, these things will happen in the law" (4.1). Eventually, after further rebukes, Law is arrested upon a "lord chief-justice's warrant" (4.1), and the conspiracy is thwarted. The manner of Law's arrest reflects Fielding's faith in the superior power of higher law, and the character of Law suggests that the true function of law within the realm has been usurped by individuals motivated solely by personal pride and ambition. The satire is carefully generalized, and good law triumphs over bad. Fielding does not condemn all lawyers; he directs his barbs against those persons who, given sufficient latitude, might easily drag the law down to the level of their own treachery. Moreover, legal abuses could not exist in a realm where legal practice is governed by common sense.

Perversion of the law is a permanent concern in Fielding's works; he never abandons his censure of those who disgrace the profession by their mean and caviling practice. His pettifoggers appear and reappear in all his novels, but one notices that they are invariably balanced by worthy lawyers who represent the finest ethical standards of professional conduct. In fact, few of his evil lawyers pose a serious threat to the major characters, for their deceit is either neutralized by the good lawyers or by the natural goodness of his heroes and heroines. The treacherous lawyer is frequently not a lawyer at all. The pestiferous Scout in *Joseph Andrews* is, as it turns out, merely "one of these fellows, who without any knowledge of the law, or being bred to it, take upon them, in defiance of an act of Parliament, to act as lawyers in the country, and are called so. They are the pests of society, a scandal to the profession, to which indeed they do not belong, and which owes to such kind of rascallions the ill-will which weak persons bear towards it."[58] Not wishing the odium of pettifoggery to cling to genuine members of the profession, Fielding makes the same distinction in his later novels, while presumably genuine lawyers like Dowling, Blifil's evil factotum in *Tom Jones,* disappear from the plot silently and ignominiously, without the dignity of further comment than their own shameful conduct.

Fielding's scornful attitude toward pettifoggery is best shown in his contemptuous dismissal of the "lawyer" who tells lies about Tom Jones to the landlady of the Gloucester Inn. This unnamed lawyer "was indeed a most vile pettyfogger, without sense or knowledge of any kind; one of those who may be termed train-bearers to the law; a sort of supernumeraries in the profession, who are the hackneys to attorneys, and will ride more miles for a half-a-crown than a post-boy."[59] Their chief business seems usually to be the kind of employment in which they serve as agitators and agents for the villainous characters. If they achieve a temporary success, they manage it only because of the innocence and naivete of characters like Parson Adams, Partridge, and Tom Jones. In other words, in his mature novels, Fielding uses the conventional representation of the pettifogger as a kind of foil to the major characters, whose inherent goodness shines the brighter because they cannot stoop to treachery and deceit. The pettifogger can only exist in a society controlled by unscrupulous and litigious individuals like the snobbish Boobys and the despicable Blifil. Although the settings have changed, the basic characterization of the pettifogger has remained constant.

An Outward and Visible Sign: The Lawyer's Busy-ness

From the very beginning, one of the hallmarks of the greedy and corrupt lawyer has been his conventional busy-ness; he never has time to listen to his clients and rushes everywhere in a frightful haste. Among the first to remark on this feature of the lawyer's representation is Chaucer, in his portrait to the Man of Law:

> Nowher so bisy a man as he ther has,
> And yet he seemed bisier than he was.
> (1, 321-22)

The remark seems innocuous enough, although it causes nagging doubts for thoughtful readers. It is no sin to be busy, or even to appear so, and the modern reader, especially one deeply indoctrinated by the Protestant work ethic, may wonder what Chaucer means. Why, of all the possible things he may have said about this Man of Law, did he choose this detail? Part of the answer lies in the verb *semed* which in Middle English had a well-known secondary meaning: "deliberately to create appearances," with a suspicion of false pretenses or perhaps of some more sinister motive. Shakespeare uses this connotation to describe the behavior of one of his famous lawyers, Angelo in *Measure for Measure*. For example, after he has invested Angelo with the office of deputy, the Duke remarks to Friar Peter, "Hence shall we see, / If power change purpose, what our seemers be" (1.3.53-54), and Angelo, once bitten by lust, laments that place and form may "wrench awe from fools, and tie the wiser souls / To thy false seeming!" (2.4.14-15). Though he may have less sinister motives than Angelo's, Chaucer's serjeant is also a man of considerable power and influence. His seeming may stem from a desire to "wrench awe from fools," a desire which in itself is no sin unless it is accompanied by the concomitant desire to wrench money and lands from them. The picture darkens slightly when we realize that the Man of Law is a great "purchasour" of lands in "fee simple." Nothing else confirms the suspicion; it simply suspends there in all it glorious possibility.

Another way of approaching Chaucer's equivocal portrait of the serjeant is to compare it with other literary portraits of lawyers. Oddly enough, legal "bisinesse" and the scramble for landed estates are usually linked in most medieval law satires. In "Money, Money," avarice and legal haste combine in the poet's description of Westminster Hall:

> In westmynster hall the criers call;
>   The sergeauntes plede a-pace;
> Attorneys appere, now here, now there,
>   Renning in every place.

> What-so-ever he be, and yf that he
> Whante money to plede the lawe,
> Do whate he cane In ys mater than
> Shal prove not worthe a strawe.[60]

The implication is that money controls the lawyer's time. If the client lacks money, the lawyer is too busy to hear him. If the client is wealthy, his cause will go on "a-pace," as fast as the lawyers can dispose of it. Langland's and Gower's lawyers are also noted for their disregard of the poor client, particularly those who must sue in forma pauperis.[61]

The outstanding description of legal "bisinesse" is the view of Westminster Hall presented in the anonymous "London Lickpenny," with its persistent refrain, "But for lack of mony, I cold not spede."[62] In this poem, the impoverished litigant visits all the courts in turn, seeking justice. In every court, he notices that everyone is too busy to heed his requests, and he even loses his hood in "the prese amonge." The scene is filled with almost headlong bustle, as the criers keep proceedings on the move. A "gret Rout" of clerks "fast dyd wryte by one assent." The lawyers sweep the poor client aside with remarks like "I wot not what thou meanest." Even at the Rolls, the Clerks of Chancery ignore him although their court was originally established to receive the bills of poor men. The remaining half of the poem details Lickpenny's return to Kent through the city of London. The refrain "for lack of mony I cold not spede" continues, linking the halves of the poem together. Such juxtapositions in medieval poems normally serve a thematic purpose, as the court and city scenes do here. In "London Lickpenny," the poet clearly intends to show that Westminster Hall is the legal counterpart of such marts as the Chepe, Cornhill, and Billingsgate. The parallel suggests that the lawyers are in fact operating a kind of law market, in which the citizen can buy nothing if he has no money. Finally, when Lickpenny sees his own stolen hood, which he had lost in Westminster Hall, on sale at Cornhill and cannot afford to buy back what is rightfully his, the moral is clear. His journey to the courts has been motivated by his desire to obtain justice, the right of any citizen at law. The hood symbolizes his right to a fair hearing, a right which has been stolen by the lawyers' greed. In modern parlance, we might say that he has "lost his shirt." The ultimate insult, a theme often used in law satire, is the comparison of the lawyers' eloquence to the fishmongers' language in the Billingsgate scene.

Medieval law satire, however, is far more sweeping in its treatment of the legal profession than the works of Tudor-Stuart critics. The literature of the Renaissance yields several portraits of good lawyers who are willing to devote time to their clients' interests. Only the pettifoggers are universally occupied by the need to create the appearance of business. The main reasons for pettifogging haste are to create an air of importance and to extract as many fees as possible in the shortest space of time. In Fletcher's *The Little French Lawyer*, La Writt, whose total business is very little, is always putting his clients off on one pretext or another. When approached, he usually complains about his lack of time:

> Yes, I am hastie,
> Exceeding hastie, Sir, I am going to the Parliament,
> You understand this bag, if you have any business
> Depending there, be short, and let me hear it,
> And pay your Fees.[63]

Busier still is Middleton's Dampit in *A Trick to Catch the Old One,* who also associates the acquisition of wealth with the maximum use of one's time. One has little difficulty in imagining his helter-skelter existence from the cascade of words tumbling from his lips:

> And now worth ten thousand pounds my Boys, report it, *Harry Dampit,* a trampler of time, say, he would bee up in a morning, and be here with his Serge Gowne, dasht up to the hams in a cause, have his feete stincke about *Westminster* hall and come home agen, see the Galleouns, the Galeasses, the great Armadoes of the Lawe, then there bee Hoyes and pettie vessells, Owers and Scullers of the time, there bee picklocks of the Time too, then I would be here, I would trampe up and downe like a Mule; now to the Judges, may it please your reverend-honorable fatherhoods: then to my Counsellor, may it please your worshipfull patience, then to the examiners Office, may it please your Maister-shippes Gentlenesse, then to one of the Clarkes, may it please your Lowzinesse, for I finde him scrubbing in his cod-piece, then to the hall agen, then to the Chamber agen—(1.4.42-55)

Artfully, the sentence does not end, for the process described by Dampit has no conclusion. The pettifogger's only use for time is its necessary value. On the other hand, the client's time is consumed in endless delays.

A closely related motif in Elizabethan-Jacobean literature concerns the lawyer's dislike of the long vacation, as demonstrated in Rosalind's answer in *As You Like It* to the question, "Who stays it still withal?" ("For whom does Time stay still?"): "With lawyers in the vacation; for they sleep between term and term, and then they perceive not how Time moves" (3.2.352-55). Lawyers, apparently, did not like holidays because they were unprofitable. As Dearage explains in Middleton's *Michaelmas Term,* when asked about the date of Master Difficult's death: "What a question's that! When should a lawyer die but in the vacation? He has no leisure to die in the Terme-time; beside, the noise there would fetch him again."[64] With no time in which to earn money, the lawyer dies of boredom.

The lawyer's haste is a constant feature of the pettifogger's typical representation in the character books. Earle's attorney is a regular busybody whose "looks are very solicitous, importing much haste and dispatch, he is never without his hands full of businesse, that is, paper." Elsewhere, the pettifogger's chief "employment is in term time; and then, like so many bees, they are very busy in sucking their clients. They have no time to think of God nor the devill then; and observe it when you will, a lawyer never dyes but in the vacation; and if death comes then with a *habeas corpus,* he is so much at leisure he cannot put in baile to the action." Samuel Butler finds that the lawyer's "pride encreases with his Practice, and the fuller of Business he is, like a Sack, the Bigger he looks. He crouds to the Bar like a Pig through a Hedge; and his Gown is fortified with Flankers about the Shoulders, to guard his Ears from being galled with Elbows."[65]

In the Westminster Hall scene of *The Plain Dealer,* William Wycherley dramatizes legal haste in a flurry of brief scenes. In fewer than eight hundred lines, seven lawyers have speaking parts, in addition to the two principal suitors, the litigious Widow Blackacre and the less than eager Manly. All the legal figures seem overwhelmed by business, especially Buttongown who has found some rich clients (3.1.240-63) and another lawyer after Manly informs his that he must sue in forma pauperis (ibid., 660-70). The theme of legal haste is admirably mirrored in the movements of Widow Blackacre, who in a state of continuous and intense agitation, flits on and off stage like a yo-yo, and who to judge by her remarks about *serjeants, trespass, barons,* and *references* has at least one cause in progress in Common Pleas, King's Bench, the Exchequer, and Chancery respectively, as the terms imply. Her hectic career, like that of Middleton's Tangle in *The Phoenix,* reflects the kind of litigious gullibility which makes pettifoggery a successful occupation.

In eighteenth-century satire, the typical busy-ness of the pettifogger remains a constant feature of his representation. In Ward's portrait, the pettifogger seems in constant motion, always placing himself as far as possible in the public eye, his pockets stuffed with innumerable papers. He has no time to read the Bible, unless paid for it, and his "business lies most in the coffee-house," as one might expect. Nevertheless, he is always on his way to Westminster, and "indeed you may find him in the Hall much oftener than he has ten times the business there, for he is one of those that loves to hear how other people's matters go, tho' it does not at all concern him."[66]

In Fielding's plays and novels, the corrupt lawyers are also always in great haste, pretending to value their time more than it is worth, yet content to remain if they can drum up any activity. Mr. Brief in Fielding's early farce, *Don Quixote in England* (1733), engages in a continuing argument with Dr. Drench as to whether the Spanish knight is non compos mentis or simply a rogue. Brief opts for the latter since it might profitably lead to an action of assault and battery. Finally, Brief himself receives a sound thrashing at the hands of Quixote and, in his reaction to the beating, indicates that he is most worried about his loss of valuable time: "I shan't be able to appear in Westminster Hall the whole term. It will be as good a three hundred pounds out of my pocket as ever was taken"

(3.15), but as we have seen in other satirical pieces, merely appearing in Westminster Hall was no guarantee of an income. One wonders just how many briefs Brief is likely to lose as a result of his injuries. Three hundred pounds for one term's work was a considerable income even for the most illustrious barristers during this period. In *Tom Jones,* attorney Dowling is briefly and typically delineated, though he must be seen as something more than an ignorant pettifogger to serve Blifil effectively. Nevertheless, in terms of several details, he might easily be placed among Fielding's family of pettifoggers. He certainly displays the conventional busy-ness of the clan. He stereotypes himself when "he declared he must be at Hereford that evening, lamented his great hurry of business, and wished he could divide himself into twenty pieces, in order to be at once in twenty places."[67] The pettifogger lawyer is customarily damned out of his own mouth.

The main lines of the satirical representation of pettifoggers, therefore, remained remarkably constant, particularly if we include the questmongers of medieval literature, from the time of Chaucer to that of Fielding. If anything, the problem worsened because, as we have already seen, the higher ranks of the profession were unable to control the numbers of attorneys, their certification, and their educational programs. Thus, given the litigiousness and gullibility of Englishmen, there was always room for the pettifogger to fuel contention and profit from civil discord. These facts underlie historical change and explain the remarkable longevity of the pettifogger's satirical representation in all the prevailing historical genres, from medieval narratives and romances, to Renaissance drama and the character books, and eventually to the verse satire and the novel of the eighteenth century. From first to last, busy-ness was the pettifogger's business.

4

Lawyers in the Case of God v. The Devil

In a profession where unbounded trust is necessarily imposed, there is nothing surprising that fools should neglect it in their idleness and tricksters abuse it in their knavery, but it is more to the honour of those, and I will vouch for many, who unite integrity with skill and attention, and walk honourably upright where there are so many pitfalls and stumbling blocks for those of a different character. To such men, their fellow-citizens may safely entrust the care of protecting their patrimonial rights and their country the more sacred trust of her laws and privileges.

Sir Walter Scott, *The Antiquary*

The Honest Lawyer

SATIRISTS HAVE USUALLY been eager to show that their attacks upon the legal profession are directed against the tricksters who abuse the law in their knavery. The moral strategy of satire is to eradicate injustices, and that purpose is defeated if criticism is misdirected or ill-founded. Such, of course, has not been the case with satirical representations of the pettifogger because he essentially dramatizes historical perception of the legal profession, even though as Dr. Ives has suggested the representation is not always particularly accurate. The point is that a satirical representation does not have to be 100-percent true; it achieves a kind of normative effectiveness if it is, at least, generally accurate, or if the satire hits the inner rather than the bull's-eye. As an advocate for a point of view, the satirist will not be deflected from his purpose by the simple presence of certain exceptions to the rule, for like the advocate, his responsibility is to win his case. On the other hand, most responsible authors would concur with Dr. Johnson's caveat to Mrs. Thrale: "Let us I beg of you," he says, "have no general Abuse; the Law is the last Result of Wisdom, acting upon publick Experience."[1] It is this reverence for the common law which has prompted even the severest critics to preface their works with praise for those lawyers "who unite integrity with skill and attention, and walk honourably upright" in their professional lives. For Gower, the lawyer "who devotes himself to the true law and honestly furthers the justice of his neighbor's complaint is, as the Psalmist sings, a man most blessed."[2] Ruggle's scholarly Musaeus in his tirade against the ignoramuses of the law acknowledges the great numbers of honest lawyers, "ingenio, pietate, doctrina praestantes, adeo vix ut invenias pares" (indeed that you can scarcely find their equals in skill, piety, and outstanding learning).[3] Ben Jonson, whose admiration for such men as Selden, Coke, and Ellesmere, is well-known, customarily puts such apologetics into the mouths of his choric characters.[4] For example, the chorus of *The Magnetick Lady* introduces a number of gossips who discuss the possible meanings of his play, and one of the women remarks, "You might as well aske me, what *Alderman*, or *Aldermans* Mate, hee meant by Sir *Moath Interest?* or what eminent Lawyer, by the ridiculous Mr. *Practice?* who hath rather his name invented for laughter, then any offence, or injury it can stick on the reverend Professors of the Law: And so the wise one will thinke" (2.Chorus.4-9). Also, in *The Staple of Newes*, Jonson's spokesman states that his condemnation of pettifoggers, the caterpillars of the law, is justified,

> For these shall never have that plea 'gainst me,
> Or color of advantage, that I hate
> Their callings, but their manners, and their vices. (4.4.137-39)

From another point of view, one might say that these speeches merely indicate that Jonson wishes to avoid another brush with the Court of Star Chamber, but surely the playwright's deep interest in the law suggests meanings beyond a pusillanimous dread of "losing his ears."[5] Types like Picklocke, Practice, Voltore, and Chev'rill are carefully generalized and clearly deserve the humiliation they reap. At the same time, because of his generally accurate knowledge of the law and the ways in which the pettifogger operates, Jonson is able to make the representative figure a secure basis for his intensive study of legal abuses. In true Augustinian fashion, he castigates the sin rather than the actual sinners. Otherwise, the old proverb fits, "*Qui capit, ille facit.*"

The works of legal apologists actually mirror the content and temper of literary apologetics. Often the critic will admit that he is attacking a minority, as Ruggle's Musaeus does when he says that he could identify "*infinitos celebrare ordinis hujus viros,*" if that were necessary.[6] Such an opinion, embedded in one of the fiercest of all satires of the legal profession, adds point to the impression gained by critics (like E. W. Ives) who feel that the profession was not overloaded with unscrupulous pettifoggers, or Herman Cohen who suggests that "the venal practitioner whom the literary men denounce was comparatively a novelty."[7] It may well be, but as Musaeus insists, he could celebrate the honest lawyers if it were necessary, *"possem si opus."* From the standpoint of the satirist, the existence of bad exceptions to the rule is sufficient reason for criticism, just as one likes to remove the rotten apples from the barrel.

Most literary men have also been cognizant of the human tendency for the less privileged to rail against the learned and prosperous men of the world.[8] Ned Ward prefaces his *A Journey to Hell* with a solemn apology "to the Learned Professors both of Law and Physick, [for] whom ... I have a peculiar Veneration, who cannot be insensible what swarms of hungry and unskilful Practisers in both Sciences there are, who fraudulently prey upon the honest Labour of the Publick."[9] Fielding usually groups the learned professions together in his satirical works, such as *Pasquin,* while making certain that his readers know the difference between the real and false "practisers."[10] The satirical focus is nearly always upon the professional cheats, however, rather than upon the profession at large. In satirical literature, it is also the law which not only supplies the norms but also the truths which ultimately determine the fates of evil lawyers and the clients for whom they weave their devious schemes. The good lawyer waits patiently in the wings, ever ready to act as the true voice of authority.

Elsewhere, the honest lawyer is a constant presence upon the stage, often as a rather characterless or semi-allegorical figure, serving as the continual reminder of those enduring values by which the villainous lawyers must eventually be judged. The Lord Chief Justice in the two parts of Shakespeare's *Henry IV* and Escalus in *Measure for Measure* are typical of this kind of balancing characterization. Representatives of higher law, they are normally called upon to restore social harmony for the idealized ruler. In tragic literature, divine retribution and the restoration of harmony have to await God's personal judgments, although natural law works inwardly to compel villains to destroy themselves. As Claudius laments in *Hamlet,* Justice prevails in this world or the next:

> In the corrupted currents of this world
> Offense's gilded hand may shove by justice,
> And oft 'tis seen the wicked prize itself
> Buys out the law, but 'tis not so above:
> There is no shuffling, there the action lies
> In his true nature, and we ourselves compell'd,
> Even to the teeth and forehead of our faults,
> To give in evidence.
> (3.3.57-64).

In comedy and satire, the author cannot wait for the day of doom; he must bring his reprisals down to earth. Although many deplore the humiliation of Falstaff, the Lord Chief Justice prevails because of what he represents. He is not merely a stage character; he is an emblem of constant and unrelenting Justice, "a judge who feareth not to minister justice."[11]

In Webster's *The Devil's Law-Case,* the nefarious schemes of Leonora and her legal agents are thwarted by the intervention of a good lawyer and an honest judge. The corrupt lawyers like Sanitonella cannot understand Ariosto, "the very miracle of a lawyer":

> One that persuades men to peace, and compounds quarrels
> Among his neighbors, without going to law.
> . . . .
> Yes, and will give counsel
> In honest causes *gratis;* never in his life
> Took fee, but he came and spake for't; is a man
> Of extreme patience; and yet all his longing
> Is to become a judge.
> (2.1.108-15)

He does not act like other lawyers of their acquaintance. Ariosto berates Sanitonella for bringing him a brief of "some fourscore sheets of paper," and he rejects Leonora's vile suit, remarking that such treachery disgraces the law:

> For lunacy, or else the devil himself
> Has ta'en possession of thee. May like cause
> In any Christian court never find name!
> Bad suits, and not the law, breed the law's shame.
> (4.1.64-67)

Much to the chagrin of the corrupt lawyers, Ariosto achieves his ambition and is elevated to the bench when the honest Crispiano, finding himself a judge in his own cause, steps down in favor of the right-minded young advocate.

An even more miraculous lawyer is Benjamin Gripe in *The Honest Lawyer* (1616). Son of Old Gripe, a usurer who has amassed a fortune by his dealings in mortgages, young Benjamin lives in a world of incredible vice and folly. He befriends the abandoned children of a reprobate who has ruined himself and his sold his wife to a bawd. The other vicious characters in the comedy include a usurping abbot who uses his monastery as a base for highwaymen, a hothead who attempts the murder of his sleeping enemy, and Griffin the attorney who plays the ambidexter between two litigants wishing to settle a lease. Not only is Benjamin, as his father admits, too charitable "to be the sonne of old Gripe,"[12] he is too incredibly good to be true, for singlehandedly he solves all the ills which threaten the harmony of his community. He reconciles the warring litigants, exposes Griffin, reunites the ruined Vaster family, unmasks the villainies of

Abbot Curfew, and even humanizes his greedy father to the point that he returns forfeited properties and money.

Other types of satire reveal the same kind of balancing between the good and evil lawyers and judges. In many of the character books, the good and bad portraits are often presented as diptychs, as in Alexander Gardyne's *Characters and Essayes,* Nicholas Breton's *The Good and the Badde,* or John Stephens's *Satyrical Essayes.*[13] In a few cases, only the good lawyer or judge is reported, as in Sir Thomas Overbury's "The Reverend Judge," Thomas Fuller's "The Good Advocate," Joseph Hall's "Of the Good Magistrate," and H. C.'s "The Character of an Honest Lawyer."[14] Even those characters of "meere" attorneys and pettifoggers which stand alone in the character books should be read as if accompanied by the idealized portrait. In the works of less skilled authors, these corresponding and contrasting characters seem like the opposite sides of a simple equation; with each item of legal conduct, one needs only to transfer it from one side of the equation, or the other, invert the sign, and each cancels the other out. The more talented writers omit the obvious and introduce sufficient variation effectively to mask the underlying correspondences. The greater interest generated by evil men impels the writer to present the good lawyer in essentially negative terms. He is good because he does *not* take bribes, because he is *not* an ambidexter, or because he does *not* prolong causes. In spite of this, it is possible to find several stirring tributes to the morally upright lawyer, such as H. C.'s honest practitioner who leaves the world like Elisha in a blaze of glory:

> In a word, whilst he *lives,* he is the *Delight* of the *Court,* the *Ornament* of the *Bar,* the *Glory* of his *Profession,* the *Patron* of *Innocency,* the *Upholder* of *Right,* the *Scourge* of *Oppression,* the *Terrour* of *Deceit,* and the *Oracle* of his *Country,* and when *death* calls him to the *Bar* of *Heaven* by a *Habeas corpus cum Causis* he finds his *Judge,* his *Advocate,* nonsuits the *Devil,* obtains a liberate from all his infirmities, and continues still *One of the long robe in Glory.*[15]

It will no doubt exercise all the Devil's ingenuity to discover what those infirmities are.

Even the Inns of Court, most often criticized for their rowdies and fantastiques, occasionally receive honorable notice. In Lupton's *London and the Countrey,* the Inns are described in glowing terms as "the *Seminaries* of Iudgement and Iustice," which

> Moralize, Civilize the younger, advance the Learned: their Founders intended the stablishing of Peace, and confirming of Religion: many things that begin with blows, and would end in blood, are by these Professors mediated, and Christian agreement made; their number, Unity, great imployment, makes them admired, to conclude, they are Rich Megazines for Law, store-houses for policy, Bulwarkes for Equity, let them ever flourish, as long as they are ... for God, their King, and Country.[16]

Since almost all the rest of the book "carbonadoes" the vice and folly of England, this tribute to the Inns is all the more remarkable. Francis Lenton, who elsewhere lampoons the typical Inns-a-Court man, writes in high praise of the Inns as centers of polite society, which provide the best possible education for gentlemen. Similarly, whereas Middleton paints a gloomy picture of legal London during Michaelmas term, Wye Saltonstall in his character of The Tearme describes it as a time for excitement and of rebirth: "the soule of the yeere," term-time is the answer to tradesmen's prayers, when all London springs to life and puts on its best face.[17] Books are newly published, crowds throng eagerly to plays, and ladies and gentlemen parade the latest fashions. The cutpurses and cony-catchers are out in force, but in the bustle and enthusiasm, only a few, like the moral Dekker, feel much inclined to look upon carefree London as the lair of the seven deadly sins.[18] If Fraud and Chicane lie in wait for them, the majority of citizens (like Lupton) trust the law as the defender of their rights and the redresser of their grievances.

In most of these examples, we see that satirists carefully balance the good with the bad, the dual framework having its roots, as already demonstrated, in the vice-virtue literature of the Middle Ages. The medieval poet had great difficulty, however, in presenting justice in anything but allegorical terms. His only other alternative was to draw upon the distant past for illustrations of judicial integrity: Joseph, Solomon, and Daniel from the Old Testament; Solon and Cato from ancient history; or King Alfred as in *The Mirror of Justices*. The legends of these emblematic justices furnish the moralist with a source of criticism against the conduct of contemporary judges and advocates. One of the most popular exempla is the story of Susannah, moralized and explicated in judicial terms in the books of vices and virtues. According to one version, Daniel's judgment "techeth foure thinges that everi juge scholde kepe": great deliberation, right understanding (*recta ratio*), due regard for clemency, and an exemplary personal life. Judicial clemency is further illustrated in the story of the woman taken in adultery.[19] Virtuous lawyers, like the unnamed good advocate in Chaucer's *The Tale of Melibee* (7.1020-34), always follow these biblical admonitions carefully. Melibee's lawyer appears among those summoned to counsel the old man regarding the vicious assault upon his daughter, Sophia, who has been left for dead. Whereas his own kin cry out for "werra," the lawyer advises deliberation and suggests that they submit the issue to legal arbitration. Although stirred by the calls for revenge, Melibee eventually listens to his wife Prudence, who quotes Solomon's maxim, "Werke alle thy thynges by conseil," advice which supports the opinion of the lawyer. It is also worth noting that when the lawyer speaks of mercy, he calls upon the biblical precedent of "the woman that was taken in avowtrie."

The analogy between divine and worldly law is often reversed where the heavenly tribunal of Christ's last judgment is described in terms of common law procedures used in King's Bench or at the Assizes.[20] One preacher makes a comparison between the plight of sinners on the day of doom and arraignment of prisoners at common law. He reminds his congregation that the accused has four possible ways of defeating an indictment in a worldly court: "he may put hym to witteneshyng of is countre"; "he may take hym to is previlege, as yiff he be a clerke"; "he may stond dombe with-owten answere"; or he may take the offensive by "vey of appell."[21] In other words, he may plead not guilty (put himself on the country), take the benefit of clergy by reading the so-called neck verse (but only on a first offense), stand dumb (in which case he would be pressed to death, yet escape the stigma of being a "condemned" felon), or appeal (accuse) someone else of the crime and face trial by battle (an early version of turning state's evidence). The preacher's analogy is effective because it reflects the juridical thinking which underlies criminal procedure, for the common law believed that it could not submit the accused person's inner motivation to human judgment.[22] In other words, the jury could determine whether a criminal act had occurred accidentally, or whether the accused had killed in self-defense, if there were eye witnesses, but no one could decide the truth of motivation in the absence of positive proofs. Only God can search the human heart and reveal the truth, either in trial by combat or by the ordeal. This belief is central to the preacher's analogy because, for the sinner who raises his hand at the bar of eternal justice, God's omniscience renders all four alternative common law pleas futile as a means of escaping conviction. Pleas of not guilty and standing dumb would be pointless in heaven, and there is even less benefit in claiming privilege of clergy; and, since God determines who wins in trials by battle and therefore does not need approvers, resort to the appeal is equally fruitless for the guilty. There was, of course, a fifth plea: to confess guilt and throw oneself on the king's mercy. In eternal jurisprudence, there is likewise only one plea that makes any sense— "*Tibi soli peccavi, et malum coram te feci*" (Ps. 1:6). Though one cannot expect a pardon, God is infinitely merciful.

Similar correspondences between divine and earthly justice play an important part in Renaissance literature, except that they are usually less explicit or are enmeshed in greater complexity. It is useful, therefore, to remember these medieval contexts when a Portia or an Isabella sues for mercy, or when with trenchant irony Shylock hails Portia as another Daniel. Tudor and Jacobean authors display a marked fondness for these traditional legal analogies. In Spenser's *The Faerie Queen,* Talus is the iron fist of justice, Mercilla the emblematic figure of equity, and throughout the poem, the law is a pervading metaphor for universal harmony.[23] Many aspects of civil and criminal law are, thus, placed against the backdrop of eternity, against which all human contracts, tenures, inheritances, and bequests blur into insignificance. In Gataker's *God's Parley with Princes* (1620), preached on Psalm 82: 6-8 at Serjeant's Inn, the message, as the subtitle suggests, is structured on the form of the appeal.

Addressing such a learned audience, the preacher naturally wishes to display his familiarity with and appreciation for legal terminology, as when he speaks of the corporate inheritance of kingdoms, alluding to feudal seigniory, the performance of homage, and the incidents of tenures: "For hee is absolute and independent. Other Kings and Princes are not absolute. They hold all from him; they depend all upon him; they doe service all to him." In God's Domesday Book, kings take a downward step in the feudal hierarchy and become tenants *in capite*.[24]

Geoffrey Bullough has shown that Donne's works are deeply influenced by his knowledge of the law, not only from his own experience at the Inns but also because of his six-year appointment as divinity reader at Lincoln's Inn (1616-1622). Donne's *Devotions,* not directed at a legal audience, is also filled with legal images and metaphors, used to describe man's precarious tenure in this world, in which all lands, chattels, and rights escheat to God, except the fateful legacy of Adam. In his sermons, Donne also uses the criminal law procedure of English courts to describe the day of judgment and to stress the impossibility of smothering evidence in Christ's Court.[25] Elsewhere Thomas Fuller shows that eternal justice is the one true source of vindication for the man unjustly accused:

> If one conceive himself wronged in the *Hundred,* or any inferiour Court, he may by a *certiorari,* or an *accedas ad curiam,* remove it to the *Kings-Bench* or *Common Pleas,* as he is advised best for his own advantage. If he apprehendeth himself injured in these Courts, he may with a *Writ of Error* remove it to have it argued by all the Judges in the *Exchequer-chamber.* If here also he conceiveth himself to find no justice, he may with an *injunction* out of *Chancery* stop their proceedings. But if in the *Chancery* he reputeth himself agreed, he may thence appeal to the *God of heaven and earth,* who in another world will vindicate his right, and severely punish such as wilfully offered wrong to him.[26]

The renaissance preacher, regardless of denomination, kept the specter of eternal judgment constantly before his congregation, lawyers and clients alike.

The human barrier, separating these jurisdictions, is death, as Hamlet recognizes in that amusing but terrifying graveyard scene. As the shadow of death hangs grimly and unsuspected over him, the prince imagines one of the skulls to be that of a lawyer:

> Where be his quiddities now, his quillities, his cases, his tenures, his tricks? Why does he suffer this mad knave now to knock him about the sconce with a dirty shovel, and will not tell him of his action of battery? Hum! This fellow might be in's time a great buyer of land, with his statutes, his recognizances, his fines, his double vouchers, his recoveries. Is this the fine of his fines, and the recovery of his recoveries, to have his fine pate full of fine dirt? Will his vouchers vouch him no more of his purchases, and double ones too, than the length and breadth of a pair of indentures? The very conveyances of his lands will scarcely lie in this box, and must th' inheritor himself have no more, ha? (5.1.98-112)

In eternal jurisprudence, as *Everyman* testifies, only good deeds count. It is this kind of reassurance which Sir Walter Raleigh relies upon after his gruesome trial for treason. Although one feels the bitterness of his view of Coke and his colleagues, Raleigh's "The Pilgrimage" sounds a note of calm resignation:

> From thence to Heaven's bribeless hall
> Where no corrupted voices brawl,
> No conscience moulten into gold,
> No forged accusers bought and sold,
> No cause deferred, nor vain spent journey,
> For there Christ is the King's attorney,
> Who pleads for all without degrees,
> And he hath angels but no fees.[27]

The crimes Raleigh lists, such as bribes, forgery, and jury-tampering, are those which normally belong to the representation of pettifoggers, not to presumably honest judges like Coke, but the details of Coke's arraignment of Raleigh for treason are only too well known; and the use of "angels" in the final line above alludes to the standard lawyer's fees of one angel (coin). Few lawyers would have disputed the superior claims of conscience, nor would they have denied that human law and order were continually threatened by the types of corruption Raleigh mentions.[28] Worldly law, administered by mere mortals, was at best but a pale shadow of God's law, but the positive law was, nevertheless, sacred in its larger terms. In Tisdale's "Divine Rhapsodie" of the law, the courts of England occupy the first and lowest stage of universal law:

> All richly hung about her flowry Stronds,
> With precious Gemmes like Sparkes of Diamonds
> Dropt downe from heaven: and is the common Hall
> Where divers Courts are kept, that unto All
> Give common Right, in Earth, in Ayre, in Seas,
> With *Royall, Peacefull,* and with *Common Pleas,*
> Whereof hereafter. But above all these,
> Ascending upward by a few degrees,
> One Court in glorious State above the rest,
> Opens her Gates equally East and West:
> Wherein the Sunne of Maiestie doth guild,
> Like Aprill Flowers in a Meddowy Field,
> Her starry Thrones of Iudgement.[29]

In these courts of Exchequer, King's Bench, Common Pleas, and Star Chamber, the wise judges sit, their understanding illuminated by the glorious light of divine justice as it filters through human conscience and right reason. There are, admittedly, evil lawyers, but they have no essential place in the scheme of God's laws. Although they may prevail for a while, these "Lunarian Changelings" and "Fire-drakes" are helpless in the crushing hand of truth.[30] As representatives of chaos, they will be cast into the outer darkness. In Middleton's works, we often find that justice prevails and that evil lawyers are rejected after brief periods of misrule. The archetypal Lawyer in *The World Tost at Tennis* rejects Deceit the pettifogger; the Prince in *The Phoenix* exposes Falso and hires Quieto to perform the exorcism of Tangle; and in *Old Law,* the king restores his aged and trusted magistrates, having exposed the follies of youthful greed and caprice. In all three pieces, a leading character speaks enthusiastically about the sacredness of the law, associating worldly courts with the eternal principles of justice.

Generally speaking, the higher ranks of the legal profession did not attract the satirical attention of Tudor and Jacobean writers; the great bulk of anti-law literature is directed at the attorneys and the solicitors. As G. W. Keeton observes, the high court judges, the serjeants, and barristers, "though they might be reproached for the law's delays, and the legal quibbles to which the profession was prone," were generously treated upon the Elizabethan stage, and "there was no disposition at all to doubt either their authority or their integrity." In fact, it may have been unwise to impugn their integrity for fear of their authority. It is only after the Stuart assault upon the judiciary, and the subsequent weakening of the law's sinews, that we find judges and senior lawyers becoming the target of satirists.[31] Even then, the satire written in the late Jacobean and Caroline periods is either decidedly second rate or inspired by political motives.

On the other hand, if we wish to find a more positive treatment of law and lawyers, we must look to a neglected genre: the personal eulogy, or panegyric. All but forgotten, except in the pages of biographical dictionaries, many of these eulogistic epigrams, elegies, and occasional poems provide the required balance to period satire, as Brian Morris has observed for seventeenth-century political satire.[32] These eulogistic poems are all the more significant when we recall that they were written by the same authors noted for the biting anti-law satire which has not been forgotten. Many of these tributes, such as George Whetstone's "A Remembraunce of Sir James Dyer," an elegy on the career of the late Chief Justice of Common Pleas, and the anonymous "Elegiecall Epistle on Sir John Davis Death," read like versified characters, with a few personal details added for the specific persons honored.[33] The latter poem, for example, praises the learned judge in terms which echo Sir Walter Raleigh's "bribeless hall," suggesting that Davies had managed to avoid all those legal sins which the great Devonshireman had attributed to Sir Edward Coke:

> Said I hee's dead? not soe; he could not die,
> But findinge that curst lucre, bribery

And puft ambition were the scarlett crimes
Of the Tribunall"'s tenants, and the times
Not suitinge with his vertue, cause his manner
Was to deserve and not desire, an honour;
Hee's sor'd aloft, where nought but virtue's prais'd,
And where base Mammon is not idoliz'd:
To that Kinge's Bench where Iustice is not gould,
Nor honours with old Ladies bought and sould;
To heaven's Exchequer, with intent to paye,
And render thence the Royall subsidaye
Of his rich spirit, which his soveraigne tooke
Without subscription, and crost Nature's booke.

Sir John Davies is not remembered as one of the great Jacobean lawyers. In fact, he was not even well thought of by his associates at the Middle Temple, where, as Manningham remarks, it was commonly supposed that Davies had won honors by currying the favor of the court.[34] References to the eternal King's Bench, to the Exchequer where final debts are paid, and to the Astraean lawyer who rises above legal abuses become conventional features of professional elegy. Only rarely does the elegist specify the reasons for his tribute, preferring to rely upon the traditional *topoi* and generalized allusions to the offices and works for which the subject is remembered. A clear exception to this rule is Denham's "Elegy on the Death of Judge Crooke," in which the poet praises Crooke as "the best of Judges in the Worst of Times" because of his dissenting opinion in *Hampden's Case* (1636) and his outspoken condemnation of the supposed legality of ship-money.[35]

Among the great lawyers of the Tudor-Stuart period were Sir Edward Coke, Sir Thomas Egerton (Lord Ellesmere), Sir Francis Bacon, and John Selden, all of whom received high commendation from Ben Jonson, who must also rank among the leading satirists of the law. According to Jonson, Coke was "*Solons selfe*," "the Strangers helpe, the poore mans aide," and his "Nations fame, her Crownes defence" (one wonders what James I's reaction might have been to this last phrase). Egerton is lauded for disregarding personal favoritism and powerful influence in searching out the justice of causes (one wonders what Coke thought of this opinion). Bacon is hailed as the "happie *Genius* of this antient pile," and the logical successor of his father, Elizabeth's first Lord Keeper (one wonders what Selden thought of this praise). Jonson's epigram to Selden records his delighted response to the publication of *A History of Tithes* ("What fables have you vext! what truth redeem'd!"), commending the style, wit, and antiquarian learning of this "Monarch of Letters" (and it requires little effort to imagine how greatly James I, Lord Ellesmere, and Bacon would have been "vext" by Selden's anti-prerogative views).[36] The intriguing aspect of these poems is that they are addressed to four brilliant, learned, but stubborn men who stood firmly upon opposing sides of continuing jurisdictional disputes, first between the Court of Chancery and the Common Law Courts, and second between prerogative lawyers and those who supported parliament, yet there is not a breath of suspicion in these poems of the antagonisms which divided these great lawyers.[37] It may very well be that Jonson recognized that none of his honorees thought differently when it came to the essential principles of justice and that jurisdictional conflicts were of less concern to the general public. As far as higher law is concerned, all these men are honorable, enlightened, erudite, and eminently to be trusted. Two decades later, such tributes accorded to men of such different political views would not have been possible.

In the later seventeenth century, as we shall see, writers were less inclined to write eulogies of lawyers. In fact, general opinion may well be epitomized in the popular epitaph "On A Lawyer":

> God works wonders now and then,
> Here lyes a Lawyer dy'd an honest man.[38]

Nonetheless, the good lawyers continue to be recognized, as in Milton's praise of Coke in the sonnet to Cyriac Skinner and in Dryden's "To My Lord Chancellor" (Clarendon) and "To My Honor'd Kinsman, John Driden of Chesterton." The latter poem in its general description of the honest magistrate provides a number of interesting parallels with earlier works, such as Webster's praise of the miraculous Ariosto in *The Devil's Law-Case*:

> Just, Good, and Wise, contending Neighbours come,
> From your Award, to wait their final Doom;
> And, Foes before, return in Friendship home.
> Without their Cost, you terminate the Cause;
> And save th' Expence of Long Litigious Laws:
> Where Suits are travers'd; and so little won,
> That he who conquers, is but the last undone:
> Such are not your Decrees; but so design'd,
> The Sanction leaves a lasting Peace behind;
> Like your own Soul, Serene; a Pattern of your Mind.[39]

The justice who promotes peace and actively composes disputes, who endeavors to save the litigants needless expense, and who refuses to use technicalities to prolong suits is the very opposite of the typical pettifogging lawyer. Dryden draws upon a long tradition of representational details to begin the tribute to his kinsman.

The moralists of the Restoration and Augustan periods were quite prepared to acknowledge merit where it was due. Sir Matthew Hale whose probity and judicial integrity were impeccable won the admiration of all but a few upstart courtiers. Particularly among the clergy he was honored and eulogized as the model judge, a man of conscience and absolute honesty. Not only was he celebrated by English divines like Burnet and Baxter, but his fame spread to America where Cotton Mather cites Hale's career as the example to be followed by all young lawyers if they wish to overcome the godlessness of the law. Like Hale, they must first learn to live by the precepts of the Bible.[40] The most able lawyer of the later seventeenth century (other than Lord Nottingham) was Sir John Holt, Recorder of London in 1686 and appointed Chief Justice of the King's Bench in 1689, a position he held until his death in 1710. Holt seems very much to have been a lawyer's judge, a man remembered for his legal attainments and his judicial decisions rather than for the publication of legal treatises. He also attracted the admiration of the humanists who elevate him above Hale for his rejection of witch-hunters, whereas Hale, the creature of superstition, participated in the notorious witch trial at Bury St. Edmunds which sent two unfortunate old crones to their deaths.[41] Holt also earned a measure of immortality as Verus the magistrate in *The Tatler,* "who always sat in triumph over, and contempt of, vice" and who "was a man of profound knowledge of the laws of his country, and as just an observer of them in his own person." Steele singles him out as a compassionate judge who always gave the criminal a fair hearing, assisting him where possible in the presentation of evidence. Following the example of the character books, the author places his portrait of the good lawyer into direct juxtaposition with the characters of Trick-Track and Tear-Shift, mere pettifoggers who compared to the great Holt are vile monkeys.[42]

William Cowper, Land Chancellor from 1707 to 1710, an honest enough man when compared with his predecessor Sir Nathan Wright or the unfortunate Lord Macclesfield a decade later, is not particularly remembered as a great lawyer. He is given lavish praise, however, as Manlius in one of John Hughes's contributions to *The Spectator,* while Steele dedicates a volume of *The Tatler* to him, and Addison praises him highly as a man of exceptional integrity in *The Spectator.*[43] During the eighteenth century, in fact, most of the great lawyers receive at least a share of the literary plaudits, although many of them are pilloried in the satire of the period. None received more critical attention than William Murray, Lord Mansfield, whose literary record reminds one of the nursery rhyme about the little girl who had a curl "right in the middle of her forehead."[44] The second half of this chapter shows the horrid side of Lord Mansfield, but, for the moment, it suffices to demonstrate that many authors thought he was very, very good. Together with Sir William Fortescue, Master of the Rolls, Murray was first immortalized by Alexander Pope who had many harsh things to say about lawyers.[45] For Pope, the young Murray was the soul of wit, the rising star of the legal profession, and a speaker whose eloquence and style surpassed the greatness of Cicero and Clarendon. He was in those early Hanoverian days a young bachelor,

> Noble and young, who strikes the heart
> With every sprightly, every decent part;
>   Equal, the injur'd to defend,
> To charm the Mistress, or to fix the Friend.[46]

Robert Lloyd in "The Law Student" is also inspired by the spirit of Lord Mansfield: "At thy name / What bosom glows not with an active flame? / Alone from jargon born to rescue Law, / From precedent, grave hum, and formal saw!" Only Mansfield, it seems, had the wit and the influence to rid the law of its chicanery and empty ceremony. In his early works, even the fiery Churchill expressed admiration for his wisdom until Mansfield showed his hostility to rakes like Wilkes and handed down a number of rather severe decisions against libellers. In a later poem, Churchill introduces Mansfield in a dual capacity, first as a monstrous enemy to justice and then, specifically by name, as an enemy to that enemy ("Bad news for our blaspheming band / Of scribblers, but deserving note").[47]

Samuel Johnson, according to Boswell, usually treated the leading lawyers of the day with deference and respect, especially men like Mansfield and Thurlow. On one occasion, however, the doctor responded rather testily to some laudatory comments about Mansfield: "Johnson, I know not upon what degree of investigation," says Boswell, "entertained no exalted opinion of his Lordship's intellectual character. Talking of him to me one day he said: 'It is wonderful, Sir, with how little superiority of mind men can make an eminent figure in public life.'"[48] Johnson, who disliked extravagant praise, even for himself, rarely let such opportunities pass by. Another poet who wrote in praise of Lord Mansfield was William Cowper, who had in his youth worked at Chapman's with Edward Thurlow, in preparation for a career in law. In 1780, during the Gordon Riots, the mob destroyed Lord Mansfield's mansion, and Cowper used the opportunity to write a eulogy to the man, his vast erudition, and the irreparable loss of his books and papers:

> And MURRAY sighs o'er Pope and Swift,
>   And many a treasure more,
> The well-judg'd purchase and the gift
>   That grac'd his letter'd store.
>
> *Their* pages mangl'd, burnt, and torn,
>   The loss was *his alone*;
> But ages yet to come shall mourn
>   The burning of *his own*.[49]

The reading of satire obviously cannot stand alone in determining literary attitudes toward the legal profession. The fullest representation of the common lawyer must also include the panegyrical verses which strike the reasonable balance, just as the character writers tried to effect an equilibrium in their portraits of vicious and virtuous lawyers. In the periods studied, the best satire, having effectiveness and persuasive power, is the work of those authors, like Ben Jonson, who have carefully drawn the necessary distinctions. Unfortunately, however, the most interesting literature on the representation of the common lawyer is not to be found in the pages of idealized portraiture and personal eulogy. For this, we must return to the pettifoggers as they are represented to us in a variety of satirical types.

The Devil's Advocates

According to Roscoe Pound, the close associations between the lawyers and the Devil was not the invention of English authors. The convention stems from the clash which occurred between the church courts and the rising class of secular lawyers in Italy during the twelfth century. Pound cites the following anecdote as an example of this nascent antagonism: "From this period proceed such stories as the one of how the lawyers prayed for a patron saint: upon papal concession that the saint whose statue a representative lawyer duly blindfolded, should select might be claimed and revered by the profession as their patron, an eminent advocate with bandaged eyes groped about the room, came upon the statue of St. Michael putting down Satan and as in duty bound embraced the statue of Satan."[50] As far as the Roman church is concerned, the Devil has always had his advocates: those used in the trial of canonization to question the saint's credentials. That such prejudices, as revealed in Pound's anecdote, scarcely diminish with time seems sufficiently evident in another story about St. Ives, who with St. Nicholas is the real patron saint of lawyers and whose emblem according to legend is a cat. The cat is appropriate, explains Baring-Gould, "being regarded as in some sort symbolizing a lawyer, who watches for his prey, darts upon it at the proper moment with alacrity, and when he has got his victim, delights to play with him, but never lets him escape from his clutches."[51] Analogies with various predatory creatures, such as foxes, ferrets, vultures, and spiders are commonplace in law satire.

Although Pound may be correct in attributing ecclesiastical motives to the initial creation of the Devil as the lawyer's patron, his theory is hardly adequate to account for the subsequent popularity of the convention in English literature. Characters in exempla of this kind are supremely interchangeable and may serve to illustrate the preacher's distaste for any profession or trade. The Summoner in Chaucer's *The Friar's Tale,* who becomes the sworn brother of the Devil only to be whisked away to hell as a result of his depravity, is a lawyer in an analogous story from the *Proptuarium exemplorum* of Johannes Holt, but for the purpose of a sermon, he could be a bailiff, steward, reeve, or even a sheriff.[52] The lawyer did not stand alone in popular ecclesiastical disfavor, and no profession was immune to charges of diabolical associations. The Devil could appear in any guise, as Chaucer's Canon's Yeoman warns,

> Withouten doute,
> Though that the feend noght in oure sighte hym shewe,
> I trowe he with us be, that ilke shrewe.
> (8.915-17)

The Devil is always in disguise, but during the Middle Ages, at least, the lawyer had not cornered the market as his favorite agent.

While it is difficult to determine the precise origins of the lawyer-devil type in English literature, the major influence seems to stem from the morality drama of the fifteenth century, in which the legal profession is virtually always on the side of vice.[53] By the time of Shakespeare, however, there was already a considerable body of literature in which the lawyer-devil was becoming conventional. In the anonymous *Woodstock*, the devilish Tresilian, Richard II's Lord Chief Justice, identifies himself in a typical vice's confession as an ambidexter:

> But yet until mine office be put on
> By kingly Richard, I'll conceal myself;
> Framing such subtle laws that Janus-like
> May with a double face salute them both.[54]

Tresilian's supposed diabolical motivation was not unknown in the historical literature of the Tudors. According to one account, the Chief Justice had tried to prevent his execution by wearing charms (*experimenta*), zodiacal signs, and images of demons on his way to the gallows.[55] Ambidextry was not only the Janus-like sin of the Vice characters; it was also a law term used in actions upon the case *pro deceptione* against lawyers, as in *Somerton's Case* (1433) brought against an attorney who had been retained to purchase a manor only to effect the conveyance of it to another party who paid a higher fee. As John H. Baker remarks, "The earliest cases were brought against lawyers for 'ambidextry,' the offence of taking fees from both sides, or for disclosing counsel to adversaries."[56] Thus, Tresilian's conduct combines the representation of the vice with a relatively common civil offence associated with lawyers.

The anonymous *Returne of the Knighte of the Poste From Hell*, like Dekker's *Seven Deadly Sins of London*, is a tract which applies the doctrine of mortal sins, and their numerous branches, to the social life of Jacobean London; but whereas Dekker generalizes his criticism of contemporary society, *The Returne* places a much greater emphasis upon legal sins. A knight-of-the-post was an individual used by unscrupulous attorneys to submit false testimony under oath, for a sizable fee. As it was firmly believed that oaths bind the soul, and as oaths were not taken lightly at this early stage of legal development, the services of these professional perjurers were of great value to the pettifoggers. The chief character of *The Returne,* however, is not simply a knight-of-the-post but a shape-shifting demon. In a long soliloquy he explains how he succeeds in inducing men to commit all the deadly sins. A difficult assignment at best, he can only accomplish it by assuming a variety of roles, but when he describes his customary disguises, we realize that they all relate in some way to the law. "Thinke you," says he, "the Devils Factors shift their shapes no ofter then wilde Irish women their smockes, O you are deceived I am a Citizen, but for Cittie occasions, as to bayle unthriftes, to defeat creditors, to abuse justice, and to cosen Innocentes. I am sometimes an Atturney, sometimes a Proctor, very often a Parrator, I have worne a Barresters gowne, and when neede requires, a cornerde Cappe."[57] The Devil makes no distinction, it appears, between the common or the civil law, or between bar and bench. The tactics he employs are similar in many respects to those used by Lincus to destroy the harmony of Daniel's Arcadia.

In Elizabethan-Jacobean literature, it is mainly in the drama that the convention of the lawyer-devil initially developed. University drama produced notable lawyer devils in the characters of the Recorder in *The Return from Parnassus* (1600), who is styled "one of the devill's fellow-commoners...one that is so dear to Lucifer," and also of Niphill in the anonymous *Club Law* (1581).[58] The convention is further developed in the popular drama and may explain the temptation and fall of Angelo in Shakespeare's *Measure for Measure,* who uses the law to manipulate his victims and whose temptation is complete when he utters the incriminating words, "Let's write 'good angel' on the devil's horn"(2.4.16). The motif underscores the superstitious conduct of the rebels in *2 Henry VI* when they resolve to kill all the lawyers, as in the case of the unfortunate Clerk of Chatham, who is executed by Cade's men for merely owning a book written in court-hand. The mob regard the legal script as certain proof of the lawyer's being in the Devil's pay (4.2.86ff.). Other diabolically inspired lawyers include Dampit in Middleton's *A Trick to Catch the Old One,* who "has been a trampler of the law, sir; and the devil has care of his footmen" (1.4.32-33); the knavish Churms in *Wily Beguiled,* plagued by a familiar in the shape of Robin Goodfellow; and Marall in Massinger's *A New Way to Pay Old Debts,* whose religion is said to be "the devil's creed" (1.1.102). Middleton also alludes to the association between lawyers and the Devil in *Michaelmas Term* when old father Michaelmas, returning from riding the circuit, dons his official robe, remarking, "Who first made civil black, he pleas'd the devil" (Prologue, 12).

A favorite variation on the lawyer-devil theme is the case of the law-distracted madman, frequently thought to be possessed by evil spirits. The best example of this type is Middleton's Tangle in *The Phoenix* (1607): "an old crafty client, who, by the puzzle of suits and shifting of courts, has more tricks and starting-holes than the dizzy pates of fifteen attorneys; one that has been muzzled in law like a bear, and led by the ring of his spectacles from office to office" (1.2.153-57). Tangle is not a professional lawyer as some have thought. He supports the great mass of his litigation by acting as a solicitor, advising other clients like himself, directing them to attorneys' offices. By strict legal standards, he would be considered a maintainer rather than a solicitor, for he was exactly the kind of supernumerary of the law whose activities had been condemned by contemporary legislation.[59] After much confusion and hysteria, during which he loses three of his most cherished causes in close succession, Tangle goes completely insane, spouting law terms in a continuing stream of gibberish. The mystic Quieto is summoned to the client's assistance by the prince, and Tangle's problem is diagnosed as diabolical possession: "Tis the foul fiend, my lord, has got within him" (5.1.285). Undertaking his cure, Quieto proceeds to exorcize him by means of incantations: "Thou shalt give up the devil, and pray; / Forsake his works, they're foul and black, / And keep thee bare in purse and back" (5.1.322-24). Ben Jonson also demonstrates his familiarity with this motif by using it in the famous trial scene of *Volpone*, when Voltore the lawyer feigns to be afflicted by devils and allows himself to undergo a mock exorcism. The antic figure of Trouble-All in Jonson's *Bartholomew Fair*, who will agree to nothing without a warrant, is another famous example of the individual who has been driven out of his wits by the harshness and complexity of the law.

The devilish lawyer or law victim possessed by demons is often made to speak in the most outlandish jargon of the trade. Lurdo in John Day's *Law-Tricks* (1608) mixes Latin and English in many of his speeches, either to intimidate the ignorant or to assert a ludicrous sense of superiority:

> *Non tenet in bocardo* I demurre,
> Do but send out your *Iterum summoneas,*
> Or *capias ut legatum* to attach,
> And bring him *viva voce* tongue to tongue,
> And *vi et armis* Ile revenge this wrong.[60]

Tangle, of course, far outshines Lurdo and uses scores of legal terms, reflecting perhaps Middleton's superior knowledge of the law. At one point in *The Phoenix*, he engages the corrupt justice, Falso, in a mock duel of legal terms, each scoring hits like fencers. Later he rages in total distraction, delivering a stream of pure nonsense: "Your *mittimus* shall not serve: I'll set myself free with a *deliberandum*, with a *deliberandum*, mark you. . . . A judgment, I crave a judgment, yea! *nunc pro tunc, corruptione alicujus.* I peeped me a raven in the face, and I thought it had been my solicitor: O, the pens prick me! . . . Away, I'll have none on't: give me an *audita querela,* or a *testificandum,* or a despatch in twelve terms: there's a blessing, there's a blessing! . . . Is't come to a *cepi corpus?* O, an extent, a proclamation, a summons, a recognisance, a tachment, and injunction! a writ, a seizure, a writ of 'praisement, an absolution, a *quietus est!"*[61] If this passage makes any sense, it must stem from a recognition of these terms' meanings, for consecutively and in rapid sequence they describe an extended trial of the spirit, in which the evil influence is arrested, dragged through the legal struggle in its many forms and ramifications, finally to be forced to judgment, or in this case submission to the will of the exorcist. The work of Quieto in purging the soul of evil influence is paralleled by the *quietus est* which ends the trial with satisfaction for all debts and damages. Middleton, a writer with a legal background, is not making a mockery of the law; he directs his satire at those who look upon the law as a mere system of procedures, who seem to regard the law as a code of empty forms, and who have forgotten the spirit of justice which animates these forms.

The satire of legal language in plays like *Woodstock, Law-Tricks, The Phoenix,* and *Volpone* must have exercised a strong influence upon the writing of Ruggle's *Ignoramus* (1614). Ignoramus and his clerks Dulman and Pecus cannot speak a half-dozen words without using legal phraseology. In fact, the lawyer's speech is so heavily interlarded with barbarisms of Latin, Law French, and English that it seems inevitable that he should eventually be taken for a witch or a devil, and Ruggle introduces a number of speeches anticipating such a conclusion. The main trouble begins when Ignoramus rants and raves at the shrew Polla, who gives him a sound Vice's thrashing for casting magic charms upon her. When Polla's husband Cupes hears this news, he is delighted and uses the misunderstanding to hatch a scheme with Trico:

> Ile tell thee *Trico,* this simple *Ignoramus*
> canting hyperboles in lawyers Rhetorick
> alias Pedlars-French, such as lawyers use
> to ev'ry person, and to ev'ry purpose
> has begot a rumour among the people
> that hee's possest with spirits; and ev'ry word
> he speakes in's Court-hand Langwage
> is taken for the name of some infernall spirit.(4.5.97-104C)

Cupes and Trico succeed in their plan by enlisting the aid of the dissolute Friar Cola, who stages a mock exorcism. Every time Ignoramus utters a legal term or phrase, the jargon is immediately misconstrued as the name of one of his supposed familiars. Finally, because of his inability to respond without using law terms, the exorcists judge him an inveterate witch and carry him off to a local monastery to be tortured with holy fire. Thus by utilizing the rumor of the lawyer's demonic possession, the wily servant and his cohorts serve the hero Antonius in freeing Rosabella from the lecherous designs of Ignoramus, who wishes to "joyn issue" with her in a falsified marriage.

Ruggle's use of this superstition demonstrates his familiarity with the old legend that the Devil speaks in an unknown language, or that he often speaks in many tongues (itself a parody of the "gift of tongues"). Middleton probably drew upon this tradition in the exorcism scene of *The Phoenix,* and Jonson certainly knew the legend, for he uses it explicitly in *The Divell Is an Asse* in the scene where Pug the demon urges Fitz-dottrel to feign possession by evil spirits. Pug instructs him, among other things, to "laugh loud, and faine six voices" (5.5.28), and his scheme nearly succeeds. When Fitz-dottrel gabbles in Greek, Spanish, and French, one of the superstitious bystanders exclaims, "It is the *divell,* by his severall languages" (5.8.121). The clearest reference to the legend occurs in Marston's *The Malcontent:* "Phew! the devil: let him possess thee; he'll teach thee to speak all languages most readily and strangely" (1.1.71-73). Marston elsewhere combines the satire of legal language and the lawyer-devil theme:

> Look, yon comes John-a-noake and John-a-style:
> They're naught but slow-paced dilatory pleas,
> Demure demurrers, striving to appease
> Hot zealous love: the language that they speak
> Is the pure barbarous blacksaunt of the Geat;
> Their only skill rests in collusions,
> Abatements, stoppels, inhibitions,
> Heavy-paced jades, dull-pated jobbernolls,
> Quick in delays, checking with vain controls
> Fair justice' course, vile necessary evils,
> Smooth seem-saints, yet damned incarnate devils.[62]

Since success at law required skillful use of legal language and of procedural technicalities, there is a certain pointlessness in attacking it, for it is a problem which will not simply disappear. That is why Marston speaks of procedures and terms as "vile necessary evils." As Benjamin Gripe warns the young orphans, when the fiery Robert Vaster swears revenge upon those who have ruined his father, "Incens'd Youth, / Thou fight'st 'gainst power with a sword of straw: / As good cope with the divell, as with the Law" (B4v).

The lawyer-devil motif occasionally appears in other forms of early seventeenth-century literature. To the moralist Edward Hake, better known for his legal writings than his poetry,[63] the evil lawyers are likened to "wandring Spriets" which "aye walcke abroade at wyll," who "turne darknesse into lyght, / and lyght into obscured sence, and arsiversie turne eche thing," and who

Enchaunteth so the peoples hartes:
   that (voyde of all remorse)
They fawne and gape, they watch and prie,
   they leaze and eft forsweare,
They worke the thing that wicked is,
   they cursse, they ban and teare
The blessed name of great *Iehove*.[64]

Their primary motivation, according to Hake, is avarice, and gold is their chief link with the devil. As Philip Stubbes remarks, lawyers are "rich indeede toward the devill and the world ... for they will not speak two words under an angell (for that is called a counsellor's fee)."[65] If they appear wise and knowledgeable in the law, it is only because the ignorant cannot recognize the truths they darken, but to the truly perceptive thinker, this wisdom is merely a pale reflection of the true light of justice, as the moon is of the sun. Their cunning depends

Onely upon the Light thy Lampe doth lend,
And wax and waine, as to and fro thy Light,
Doth come and goe, not shining but by Night,
In darknesse for their owne advantage sake,
And not in publike: what else can we make
Of them but Antikes, or strange Mimick Apes,
That in oure daunce can put on any shapes,
And yet be nothing?[66]

In the light of sacred law, Tisdale's corrupt lawyers are clearly on the Devil's side and are, therefore, only illusory shapes, non-beings, in the divine hierarchy of the law.

A constant theme of the character writers is the pettifogger's lack of religion and conscience. Earle's attorney never gives any thought to his soul's health because "his businesse gives him not leave to thinke of his conscience, and when the time or tearme of his life is going out, for Doomes-day he is secure, for hee hopes hee ha's a tricke to reverse iudgement." For Stephens, the attorney's religiosity is usually hypocritical, for although he often commends divinity, he acts superior to it and "still preferres the authority of a Statute where it makes for his purpose (though mistaken) before God and a good conscience. And he would willingly come to Church on Sundaies if he had ended his Declarations." Overbury's lawyer worships the law and believes "no way to heaven ... so wise as through Westminster-Hall; and his Clarks commonly through it visite both heaven and hell. Yet then he oft forgets his journeys ende, although he looke on the *Starre-chamber*." Webster's pettifogger, although "he feares not God," is "a

Vestrie man in his Parish, and easily sets his neighbours at variance with the Vickar." He desires but cannot abandon "the reverend Service in our Church, because it ends with *The peace of God*."[67] Presumably he is powerless to raise a disturbance against the *pax Dei* because it technically coincides with the *pax regis,* or because it "passeth all understanding." Underlying the traditional representation of the pettifogger, including his business and his deliberate fomentation of civil strife, is a basic disdain for the laws of God.

A full review of all the humble remonstrances, pitiful outcries, and doleful lamentations of the Puritans, in sermon and pamphlet, would yield thousands of references to diabolical lawyers. Their consistent thesis reiterates Luther's dictum, *Juristen böse Christen, ja diabolisten,* and their almost invariable recommendation for reform of the law was "Abolish it!"[68] The general view of the radicals, such as the Diggers, Levellers, Fifth Monarchy Men, Anabaptists, and other assorted chilialists, can quickly be summed up in the words of Gerard Winstanley:

> And the plain truth is, thieves and murderers (upheld by preaching witches and deceivers) rule the nations: and for the present, the laws and government of the world are laws of darkness, and the devil's kingdom, for covetousness rules all.... the attorneys and priests and lawyers and bailiffs are servants to Beelzebub, and are devils; their prisons, whips, and gallows are the torments of this hell, or government of darkness; for mind it all along, and you shall see that covetousness and bitter envy gets freedom by these laws; but the sincere and meek in spirit is trod underfoot.[69]

Winstanley sets himself up as the spokesman for the poor, who could not expect equal treatment before the law. If in their penury poor men steal to avoid starvation, he asks, do poor men deserve hanging any more than lawyers, clerks, and judges who every day take exorbitant fees and influence-money? "Well," snorts Winstanley, "this shews that if this be law, it is not the law of righteousness; it is a murderer, it is a law of covetousness and self-love; and this law that frights people and forces people to obey it by prisons, whips and gallows is the very kingdom of the devil and darkness which the creation groans under at this day."[70] Nothing much has changed in the substance of law criticism. Everything set forth by Winstanley reflects the same complaints voiced by critics like More, Barclay, Stubbes, and Crowley a hundred years before. What has changed is the urgency and temper of the criticism—its indiscriminate vehemence.

Many of the attacks on the legal profession stemmed from the radical belief that the lawyers had thrown their support to the royalist and episcopal factions, as shown in Winstanley's listing of Beelzebub's servants: "the attorneys and priests and lawyers and bailiffs." Lucifer in *News From Hell, Rome, and the Inns of Court* (1641) expresses delight that the realm is being oppressed "by the invincible oppressing power of our children the lordly bishops, the multitude of servants, corrupt judges, base-minded lawyers, seditious attornies, and wooden-headed doctors of our civil law, proctors, prothonotaries, registers, advocates, sollicitors, and apparators, whom we have caused to swarm, like to Egyptian locusts, over all the land, for the sowing of discord, and blowing the coals of contention amongst all the inhabitants of the same."[71] Even the title suggests that there is a conspiracy between the Inns and the Roman Catholic "underground." The Devil is working his purpose out as year proceeds to year, with the expert assistance of William Laud and the common and civil lawyers. In the minds of the Levelers, the common law was the instrument of tyrannous and usurping kings, going back to William the Conqueror. As long as the common law remains the law of the land, Englishmen will live in slavery under the Norman yoke.

It was partly for this reason that reformers continued their strident assault upon legal jargon until the Rump passed a law in 1650 stipulating that all legal documents and books must be written in English and in ordinary handwriting rather than court-hand.[72] Mercurius Rhadamanthus, the "Chief Judge of Hell" who published a series of papers exposing his brethren of the long gown, was particularly delighted by parliament's abolition of Law French and Latin. He offered the following piece of doggerel to celebrate the triumph:

> The Pedlars French is altered quite,
>   The Canting tongue translated,
> The language of the Romish beast
>   Into true English stated.
>
> Thus *Babels* Tower is tumbled down,
>   Her stately Pride defaced,
> The Norman Chair quite overthrowne,
>   Their Tyranny abased:
>
> And Justice now's call'd home againe,
>   That long agoe was sent
> (By tyrant Kings, and bribed Knaves)
>   Into base banishment.[73]

The reform party had taken another giant step in the direction of Henry Robinson's cookbook of the law. The infernal judge goes on to remark that Latin ("the language of the Romish beast") is only beastly in the foul mouths of the lawyers: "The Latine tongue is good, so is Wine good in a clean vessel, but nought out of a Piss-pot."[74] This pious sentiment must have been of some consolation to Milton. After the Restoration, Law French and Latin, not to mention court-hand, were reinstated and continued to absorb the attention of satirists until they were finally abolished in 1731-1732.[75]

Meanwhile, the motif of the lawyer-devil became a convenient weapon of political satirists whose attacks upon high-ranking judges were based largely upon factionalism and sectarian prejudices. The chief devils of the next forty years, depending upon whose side one was on, where Lords Clarendon, Scroggs, and Jeffreys, the subjects of a series of "kick-'em-while-they're-down" poems, often deserved. After the Restoration, Clarendon, popularly styled "this Wiltshire hog," became increasingly unpopular to all sides. Disappointed Cavaliers disliked him because they did not receive their long-expected rewards, and the Puritans reacted violently to such pieces of legislation as the Uniformity Act (1662) and the hated Conventicle Act (1664). Thus, the Lord Chancellor paid the price of a neutral policy, and he was finally removed from office by Charles II in 1667. Before he went into exile, his dismissal was urged in such hopeful poems as the following, which proclaims the rights of the "wither'd Cavaliers":

> Break up the coffers of this hoarding thief:
> There millions will be found for their relief.
> I've said enough of linsey-woolsey Hyde—
> His sacrilege, ambition, lust, and pride.[76]

The deadly sins committed by the "devilish" Scroggs, by almost common consensus, far outweigh those ascribed to the unfortunate Clarendon. In large measure, the hard-drinking, profligate Scroggs achieved a notoriety which well deserved the scathing satire heaped upon him, while Sir George Jeffreys, chiefly for his role in the Bloody Assizes, has achieved an infamy second to none in the history of criminal law. Not surprisingly, both judges were popularly thought of as the devil's agents. In "A Westminster Wedding of the Town Mouth," Jeffreys is lampooned for marrying a shrewish woman who is compared to the Devil's dam, the ideal partner for the diabolical judge. Unfortunately, because of this infernal torment, Jeffreys now vents even greater wrath upon the innocent wretches whose misfortune it is to sit on his juries:

> He has a ven'mous heart and tongue,
> With vipers, snakes, and adders hung,
> By which in Court he plays the fury,
> Hectors complainants, laws, and jury.
> His impudence has all laws broken.

Among the laws Jeffreys broke is the act passed in 1668 to prevent the intimidation of juries, but men like Jeffreys and Scroggs wielded considerably more power than such earlier judges as Keeling and Tyrrel, at whom the statute had been originally aimed.[77]

Scroggs was also the subject of numerous attacks both upon his personal and public life, in his lifetime and long after. He was notorious for his cold-hearted and savage conduct on the bench, although contemporary satirists place greater stress upon his pro-Catholic leanings. He is ranked with the Jesuits in "Justice in Masquerade" for his diabolical cunning, and his career in "Lampoon on Lord Scroggs" is linked with that of the legendary Tresilian:

> You'll hang at the last, as Tresilian before yee;
> A judge for the Devil, a judge for the Pope,
> Begun by the cleaver, must end by the rope.

"The cleaver" alludes to the fact that Scroggs was the son of a butcher and may also refer to the old superstition that butchers were not allowed to sit on juries.[78]

During the eighteenth century, both Jeffreys and Scroggs became the stock figures in poems and prose pieces which introduce a new and interesting variation upon the lawyer-devil theme. These popular burlesque works describe apocalyptic visions of the day of doom, with reports of tribunals conducted in hell to determine the fates of lawyers. Many of these pieces involve journeys into hell, descriptions of trials and pleadings, and the prescription of torments to fit the various crimes. The trials take place in conventional settings and frequently reintroduce the same basic set of characters, such as the three judges of hell. A much earlier work in this vein, though dealing with political rather than legal figures, is the anonymous *Hell's Higher Court of Justice* (1661) in which a trial is held to determine which of three sinners (Cromwell, Mazarin, or the king of Sweden) is the wickedest. With the infernal Machiavelli presiding over proceedings which parody the High Court of Justice during the Protectorate, Cromwell wins (or loses) hands down.[79] In Charles Gildon's *Nuncius Infernalis* (1692) we also find a generalized attack upon all the learned professions, although in the "Session of Cuckolds," the lawyers play a prominent part. The court is presided over by an irritable and impatient Lucifer, and the lawyers do not fare well when they try to evade damnation by using various procedural technicalities.[80]

The next poem in the sequence, Ned Ward's *A Journey to Hell* (1700), also presents a general rather than a legal vision of hell, in which the clergy, physicians, and politicians all come under satirical fire. Nonetheless, the legal profession is given a long canto all to itself. As they are rolled into the Devil's court in Tyburn carts, the lawyers appear before Rhadamanthus who conducts his proceedings "like an old *Bridewell*-judge."[81] Speaking the devil's many languages, the laywers "murmur in a noise of strange tumultuous Tongues." They are carefully segregated according to rank, from the "Grave Robes and Gowns" of the judges and counselors down to the lowest riffraff of tipstaves and hangmen. All take their turn at the bar, undergo arraignment, conviction, and sentencing before a host of demons comes in to escort them to their various places of punishment. All the normal abuses of the lawyer's satirical representation are introduced in the course of the trial: bribes, extortionate fees, prolonging of suits, forging wills and other documents, the overuse of tautology and oversized writing to increase the numbers of pages (and fees) of jointures, indentures, and wills, plus the sins of packing and tampering with juries, the intimidation of clients, and the use of obscurities to the confusion of clients. In the charges made against and account given of each class of lawyer, or court official, the descriptions are carefully generalized, with the only names mentioned being those of stock figures of the underworld, such as the boatman Charon and the dog Cerberus.

In several of these works, however, one finds a growing genealogy of evil lawyers dating back to Tresilian, Bacon, Bradshaw, Jeffreys, and Scroggs, all condemned for twisting justice to suit the Devil's purposes. The regicide John Bradshaw, who presided over the High Court of Justice which condemned Charles I, makes his first appearance in a political vision of hell, *Poor Robin's Dream* (1681), where we discover him with Cromwell (old Noll), Ireton, and Pride "burning like Beacons,"[82] The same cast of characters reappears in a later poem, "The Devil in a Whirlwind at Westminster Hall" (1712), which relates the strange occurrences of a hurricane which swept through the courts. The fury of the blast "made each Lawyer soon to leave his Cause, / And sadly dreading that the Judgment Day / Was come, they nimbly striv'd to run away." The storm mysteriously did no other damage than to smash the commemorative busts of Bradshaw, Ireton and Noll ("the Heads of those great Sons of Shame"). Although the lawyers escape devastation, the poem leaves no doubt that the profession shares in the guilt of Charles's martyrdom by having permitted these busts to remain in place in Westminster Hall.[83] In his "A Faithful Narrative of What Passed in London" (1720), a satire based upon Whiston's prophecy that the millenium would begin in 1766, Jonathan Swift describes the general alarm which enervates the city on the eve of doomsday. Among all the citizens,

> the alarm among the lawyer's was inexpressible, though some of them, as I was told, were so vain to promise themselves some advantage in making their defence, by being versed in the practice of the earthly courts. It is said, too, that some of the chief pleaders were heard to express great satisfaction, that there had been but few state trials of late years. Several attorneys demanded the return of fees that had been given the lawyers; but it was answered, the fee was undoubtedly charged to their client, and that they could not connive at such injustice, as to suffer it to be sunk in the Attorneys' pockets. Our sage and learned judges had great consolation, insomuch as they had not pleaded at bar for several years; the barristers rejoiced in that they were not attorneys, and the attorneys felt no less satisfaction, that they were not pettifoggers, scriveners, and other meaner officers of the law.

The indefatigable dean, who among Augustan satirists seems to have entertained a particular and personal dislike for lawyers, makes certain that the entire profession is condemned for its hypocrisy, quibbling, and arrogance.[84]

Even more intriguing is *Hell in an Uproar* (1725), a dream vision describing a trial in hell to decide whether the lawyers or the physicians have better served the Devil. Like Ward's *A Journey to Hell,* this entertaining poem belongs within the genre of mock-Aeneids, except that it concentrates solely upon the legal profession since the doctors play no vital role in the satire.[85] The lawyers plead their cause first and do such a thorough job that the physicians concede in despair. In presenting their case for diabolical supremacy, the lawyers are instructed by Minos to "open one by one, / The Knavish tricks, when Mortals, they had done." The parade of witnesses includes Sir Robert Tresilian, "who had an ancient Stander been in Hell"; William Prynne, "for Crimes which did my haughty Humour puff, / I lost my Ears, and wore a Wooden Ruff"; John Bradshaw, "I judg'd my lawful King, and doomed Fate / To stop his Breath before his Palace Gate"; Sir William Scroggs, "bribes I ador'd, to rich Men lent an Ear, / Th'oppressed poor Man's Cause would never hear"; Sir George Jeffreys, "I'm sure on Earth I've done enough to make / The Devil love a Lawyer for my sake"; and finally, a certain "W___t," whom I take to be Sir Nathan Wright, the Lord Keeper from 1701 to 1705, who is interrupted immediately by Aeacus. Defoe, incidentally, epitomizes Wright's reputation (along with Forde Grey) in *The True-Born Englishman* (1701) in terms which anticipate his selection as a spokesman for the diabolical lawyers in *Hell in an Uproar:*

> They rule so politickly and so well,
> As if they were Lord Justices of Hell,
> Duly divided to debauch Mankind,
> And plant Infernal Dictates in his Mind.[86]

In the later poem, besides citing the most infamous and diabolical facts of these lawyers' careers, the anonymous versifier provides additional color with more general and topical criticism of the legal profession. Rhadamanthus summarizes the infernal judgment of lawyers in his closing verdict:

> But now to give the *Lawyers* their full weight
> Of praise, for Knavery, they win the Plate
> . . . .
> The *Templars, Lincolns-Inn,* and *Grays-Inn* Sparks
> Are very fit to make the Devil Clerks,
> Therefore they must take the place of you, and be
> The next to *Jesuits,* for Villany.[87]

A decade later appeared a prose work entitled *Law Visions; or, Pills for Posterity* (1736), another long dream vision in which the narrator makes a series of visits to the underworld to witness the continuing trial of the legal damned.[88] As in other mock-Aeneids, the dreamer describes his journeys into hell, his encounters with Charon, Cerberus, and his passage across the land of death. He accompanies the souls as they approach the place of trial and witnesses the types of punishment awarded the various representational crimes. The work has additional interest since it devotes considerable space to the individual trials of sinners like Skinall, Dick Double, Peter Puzzlecause, and an unnamed judge, thus providing a criticism of the various levels of the profession. Also of great interest is a lengthy debate to decide "whether an honest lawyer ought to plead, or might, *salva Conscientia,* plead a bad or dishonest Cause."[89] Each prisoner tries a different approach to evade the eternal judgments. Puzzlecause has managed to have himself put first on the trial list, but Minos sets aside his trial suspecting some fraud. Eventually, when he does come to trial, further witnesses appear who explain that they misunderstood the writ summoning them as witnesses. Even though he attempts all manner of evasions, the testimony of the new witnesses is damning to Puzzlecause's cause. Skinall's indictment is six yards in length. In fact, "the evidence was so full, that *Skinall* was put to his whole Troop of Evasions and Quibbles; notwithstanding all which, the Judges unanimously decreed him Tantalus's Punishment, only changing the Element of Water into that of Fire."[90] Double is accused of taking bribes and "eloping" his cause. He nearly succeeds in clearing himself until Aeacus directs a search of his body, whereby the officers discover the stinking and incriminating document "between a pair of Cheeks, somewhat more fleshy than those near his Forehead." Minos is so enraged by Double's duplicity that he commits the pettifogger to his horned janissaries to be assigned a punishment which takes the narrator a half-page to describe.[91]

Unlike many of the other works in this sequence, *Law Visions* shows some knowledge of the law and of recent legislation aimed at reform. In addition to this, the author seems particularly eager to establish models of good conduct for the profession. The three infernal judges explain points of law to the prisoners, expound the meaning of forms, and even the court crier, who befriends the dreamer, contributes a share of the commentary. When the haughty judge objects to responding to a long list of interrogatories ("such Interrogatories were never exhibited to a Person of his Rank before"), the crier answers, "Yes, yes ... *Hales* and *Holt*—will tell you they answer'd to the same; *if you ever get to speak with them.*" Later, in the debate scene, Cicero and Demosthenes are invited to be spectators and commentators on the reasoning used in the infernal moot. When the common lawyers object that the classical legists are unqualified to judge English jurisprudence, Cicero explains that their knowledge of English law is based upon long conversations with Bacon, Hales, Holt, and Finch (Lord Nottingham).[92] In its individual divisions and argumentation, *Law Visions* presents a number of issues and problems for reform without either being obvious or merely programmatic.

Much wilder and more abusive is *The Causidicade* (1743), which presents another debate among lawyers in a setting that contains apparent echoes of Milton's account of the council of Pandemonium. Styled a "Panegyri-Satiri-Serio-Comic-Dramatical Poem," *The Causidicade* in its twenty-nine pages of horrid doggerel describes the election of an "Inquisitor-General" (i.e. solicitor general), with the meeting chaired by the lord chancellor (presumably Lord Hardwicke). Like *Hell in an Uproar,* this poem (if it may be graced with that title) proceeds with each candidate setting forth his claims to infamy and ignorance in what is patently a thinly disguised attack upon the leading lawyers of the day. The successful candidate "M__" (Murray) is the same Lord Mansfield eulogized so often by greater poets.[93] It is also Lord Mansfield who figures as the enemy to justice in Churchill's *The Ghost* and who stars as the central character in John Hall-Stephenson's mock-Aeneid, *A Fragment of an Epic Poem* (1776). While visiting hell, the chief justice has free access to all the chambers with his golden rod, and, on his way to see George II, his spiritual father, he passes that area of hell set aside for lawyers:

> A dreadful cave now struck his soul with awe,
> Here were the baleful caverns of the law.
> Blue lightnings issued forth, and from within,
> His ears are harrow'd, with terrific din,
> Chains, lashes, creaking wheels, and crackling bones,
> Yells, horrid shrieks, and everlasting groans!
> Before the entrance two grim monsters lay:
> With many monster cubs in snarling play:
> Chicane the dam; and Rapine was their sire.[94]

Terrified by all this Miltonic phantasmagoria, threatened by those "Hell-hounds" with tails like hooded snakes, Mansfield attempts a hasty retreat but is arrested by the hollow, broken voice of none other than Sir Francis Bacon. The specter warns him to remember the "relentless vengeance" which awaits those who use the law for personal and political aggrandizement. Mansfield does not stay to discuss the matter but scurries off to find George II, who, as it turns out, will have nothing to do with him.

Judging from these satires, lawyers could not expect to fare well in the eighteenth-century afterworld. Because of their contribution to the world's evils, there is never much doubt about the eventual disposition of their souls. They are invariably rejected at the golden gates, and even hell at times seems overpopulated by lawyers. Charon, in Fielding's, *The Author's Farce* (1729), informs a director that if he is a lawyer, he cannot ferry him across the Styx. The devil has given him strict instructions not to admit any more lawyers because the kingdom is already too full of them.[95] Usually, the lawyer exercises great ingenuity in attempting to escape the inevitable. In "The Lawyer and the Chimney-Sweep," the lawyer is lying in bed planning a new sin to commit after he has recovered from his fit of gout. He is far from thinking that his end is near, when all of a sudden the chimney sweep's boy tumbles into his room, bawling, "My master's a-coming to give you the brush."

> "If that be the case," said the cunning old elf,
>   "There's no time to lose—it is high time to flee,—
> Ere he gives me the brush, I will brush off myself—
> If I wait for the devil—the devil take me!"

The lawyer gives himself the brush, however, when he falls down the stairs and breaks his neck, "And thus ran to the devil by running away."[96] The perfect capstone to the history of the eighteenth-century lawyer-devil is provided by the story of Flaw, an old attorney who receives notice to "quit the world." He wants to gain admission to heaven, "Tho' great from Courts of Law the distance, / To reach the Court of Truth and Justice." He also realizes that he has little hope, there being no precedent for such actions, for "'Tis said (without ill-natured leaven) / 'If ever Lawyers get to Heaven, / It is surely by slow degrees.'" Flaw, nevertheless, resolves to make the effort since he knows that St. Peter is a fair-minded judge of merit whose natural charity might be prevailed upon. The heavenly Porter has different ideas, however, concerning Flaw's suitability for eternal bliss and explains his negative decision, in terms of precedent:

> Yet never having heard there entered
> A Lawyer, nay, nor one that ventur'd
> Within the Realms of Peace and Love,
> He told him mildly to remove,
> And would have clos'd the Gate of Day.

Flaw, not so easily daunted, makes a forcible entry by taking advantage of St. Peter's good manners. The poem ends with the old pettifogger delivering the challenge, "Eject me, Peter, if you can." Though we learn no more of Flaw's fortunes, one can quite imagine how his appeal to the principle of seisin was adjudicated in heaven. Possession is presumably not nine-tenths of the eternal law.[97]

General comments on the diabolical associations of lawyers abound in the morally-centered literature of the eighteenth century. In *The Pettifoggers* (1723), a poem satirizing all ranks of the profession, lawyers are described as the devil's factors:

> So Satan lays his Wiles and Snares,
> And by Degrees for Nets prepares

> Th' unwary, whom he sure decoys,
> By Stratagems at last destroys[98]

Defoe suggests a similar skill for diabolical trickery and commends evil lawyers to the pillory as a suitable punishment, because they "employ Engines of Infernall Wit, / Cover'd with Cunning and Deceit: / Satan's Sublimest Attribute they use, / For first they Tempt, and then Accuse." The lecherous Justice Squeezum in Fielding's *The Coffee House Politican* (1730), who has taken bribes and protection money from bawds, finds that he cannot escape final humiliation unless the devil "will assist his very good friend at a crisis."[99] Again in *The Lawyers Disbanded* (1745), the hotchpotch regiment (still called the "Devil's Own") raised at the Temple to defend London against the Jacobean rebels, is quickly dismissed because

> 'Tis conjectur'd the Statesman foresaw the great Evil,
> And that raising the Lawyers, was raising the D—l;
> That their Discords, Demurrers, and Wranglings would harm Ye,
> And cause Suits and Dissentions quite thorough the Army.[100]

From one point of view, Bonnie Prince Charlie was preferable to Merry Old Nick.

Examples of this kind, furnishing satirical jibes at lawyers of all ranks, famous and infamous alike, can be endlessly multiplied from all forms of literature. One also remarks in the period from 1670 to 1750 an increasing incidence of abusive attacks upon particular individuals, although most of these personal attacks may safely be accounted for by religious and political factionalism, and move *beyond* the representations of the common lawyer which comprise the central focus of this study. A great deal of this factionalist satire is indiscriminate and ill-deserved, especially when little distinction is made between men like Scroggs and Bacon. The only genuine linkage between such disparate historical characters, indeed, is the satirical convention of the lawyer-devil type.

5

Satirical Representations
Lovers and Fools

A Civilian

A lusty ole grown-grave gray-headed Sire,
Stole to a wench, to quench his lusts desire;
She ask'd him what profession he might be?
I am a Civil Lawyer, girle, (quoth he).
A Civil Lawyer Sir! you make me muse,
Your talk's too broad for civil men to use:
    If Civil Lawyers are such bawdy men,
    Oh what (quoth she) are other Lawyers then?

Anon., Wits Recreation

Lawyers in the Grip of Cupid

MANY AN OLD SONG equates lovers and fools. Since lawyers are often depicted as ignoramuses in satirical literature, it seems logical that they should often find themselves struggling in the unfamiliar nets and snares of love. In fact, they manage to entangle themselves with alarming frequency, not only as unsuccessful and deceived lovers but also as the victims of what A. P. Herbert has described as "holy deadlock," If the lawyer is artful and skilled in argumentation, his abilities are strangely neutralized in the field of love. He enters the romantic lists at his own peril. As Wisemore in Fielding's *Love in Several Masques* observes, love-making is as tricky as the law itself, and he accuses women of being more cunning than lawyers: "You gild your deceit, and lead us to misery, whilst we imagine ourselves pursuing happiness" (4.2). Without any indebtedness to Locke, most literary lawyers equate this pursuit of happiness with property, yet a surprising number squander all they possess upon romantic interests. Others like the civilian of the epigraph achieve a notoriety only for bawdy behavior. Lecherous characters, like Fielding's Squeezum, may believe that "whoring is as methodical as law," but the only predictable element in such affairs is that they become precedents which future generations of literary lawyers fail to observe. For the representative lawyer of the satirical world, love and marriage invariably lead to disaster. Only a few, like Father William, derive any benefit from their miseries:

> "In my youth," said his father, "I took to the law,"
> And argued each case with my wife;
> And the muscular strength which it gave to my jaw,
> Has lasted the rest of my life."[1]

The rest discover that they have arrived in hell, or purgatory, before their allotted time.

In medieval literature, lawyers do not customarily rank either among the romantic or the lecherous. High romance, or courtly love, was the exclusive domain of the knighthood, even though Andreas Capellanus tries to make a case for priests. Bawdy literature, on the other hand, rarely admits the intrusion of a legal personality and draws its main characters either from the ranks of the clergy (monks and friars) or from the lower rungs of society (smiths, tradesmen, and petty merchants). An occasional figure like the lust-driven Appius in Chaucer's *The Physician's Tale* is the exception that proves the rule. In later satire, the lawyer assumes some of the traditional venality of the morality vice, but one looks primarily to continental sources for the genealogy of the lawyer-lover. The typical verse-writing amorous lawyer of Renaissance literature combines the *advocatus,* the *senex amans,* and the pedant types and is based upon the parody of Petrarchan love conventions. The aged Cleandro in Gascoigne's *The Supposes,* a suitor and a pedant, introduces the Italian convention upon the English stage, and continental representations of the advocate, merging with elements of venality and estates satire, are rapidly anglicized to produce such characters as Whetstone's Harpax (*Promos and Cassandra*), Churms in *Wily Beguiled,* Jonson's Mr. Practice (*The Magnetick Lady*), Bartolus in Fletcher's *The Spanish Curate,* the pander Knaves-Bee in Webster and Middleton's *Anything for a Quiet Life,* and the title character of Ruggle's *Ignoramus.* With a slight variation, La-Writt in Fletcher's *The Little French Lawyer* combines the *advocatus* and the miles gloriosus. In all these comedies, the lawyer poses a sexual threat to a virtuous heroine or wife, but attempted seductions invariably fail, and the lawyer undergoes some form of humiliation, either by receiving beatings from scolds or angry husbands or, like Bramble in Chapman and Jonson's

Eastward Hoe, by joining the numberless ranks of Elizabethan-Jacobean cuckoldom.

The lechery of literary lawyers is given additional point by the numerous accounts of the immoral and riotous conduct of law students and their cronies at the Inns of Court and Chancery. Shallow's reminiscences of his wenching days at Clement's Inn seem typical: "You had not four such swingebucklers in all the Inns a' Court again; and I may say to you, we knew where the bona robas were and had the best of them all at commandement."[2] Falstaff tells us that the justice's tales are purely fictitious, but he admits that young Robert Shallow had been a lecherous little fellow and confirms the general picture of student life at the Inns. As Throte informs us in *Ram-Alley,* no decent lady would dare to be caught in the vicinity of the Inns at night.[3]

In these respects, the legal world was probably no worse than the rest of Elizabethan-Jacobean society. The lawyers and students were men of their age, and, like the rest of humanity, they often set their sights higher and looked for honorable marital ties. Nor is it surprising that the legal world should be fired by the current romantic vogues and some effort would be made to adapt love conventions to legal (and illegal) aspirations.[4] Unfortunately the first attempts to accomplish his feat resulted in a string of rather badly written love elegies and the absurdities of the sonnet sequence *Zepheria* (1594). Written by an unknown author, these sonnets represent the first attempt to translate the language of courting into that of legal pleading. In these poems, the mistress is regaled with law terms. The lover's pen is his "hearts solicitour," his sonnets "faithfull counsellers" to present the "breviat" of his case. The poet brings suit, contemplates his "long adiournments," bewails his long delays and suspended sentences, threatens to remove his case by certiorari, or to sue "in conscience" and equity. Not all the sonnets in the *Zepheria* sequence follow this pattern, but most contain some allusion to legal procedure, and several are heavily laden with legal freight.[5]

Zepheria and other such productions must have created an indelible impression upon the offended sensibilities of the literati, for they soon become the butt of much satire directed against the use of legal jargon in love poetry. Not to be classified with the toothless satire of its Horatian source, John Donne's "Satyre II" features a lawyer, Coscus, who fancies himself as a love poet, who

> throws,
> Like nets or lime-twigs, whereso'er he goes,
> His title of Barrister on every wench,
> And woes in language of the Pleas and Bench.[6]

The fiercest assault upon the absurdities of *Zepheria* comes from Sir John Davies in his *Gulling Sonnets,* in which the worst faults of legal lovemaking are greatly exaggerated and lampooned. Sonnet 5 is written in the form of a legal document, replete with the usual tautologies, and sonnet 9 explores the poet's tenurial relationship to his mistress, as it proceeds from "knightes service" to that special kind of wardship in which the mistress must "holde my witte now for an Ideott." In the following poem, the object of these satirical jibes is directly identified:

> My case is this, I love Zepheria brighte,
> Of her I hold my harte by fealtye:
> Which I discharge to her perpetuallye,
> Yet she therof will never me acquite.
> For now supposinge I withold her righte,
> She hath distreinde my harte to satisfie
> The duty which I never did denye,
> And far away impounde it with despite:
> I labor therefore iustlie to repleave
> My harte which she uniustly doth impounde,
> But quick conceite which nowe is love's highe Shreife
> Retornes it as essoynde, not to be founde:
> Then which the law affords I onely crave
> Her harte for myne in wit her name to have.[7]

It is small wonder that his mistress thinks he has become non compos mentis, for his tedious analogies render his pleadings as dull and as prolix as a Chancery suit.

In Jacobean literature, the satire of legal lovemaking continues unabated, long after the vogue of *Zepheria* had sunk into merciful oblivion, for within a decade this kind of satire had become a standard feature of the lawyer's representation. Sir Thomas Overbury pillories his "meere" attorney for using legal terms in his love letters which are "stuft with *Discontinuances, Remitters,* and Uncore *prists*"; when being given leave to "speake in proper person, he talks of a French hood, in steed of a Joynture, wages his Law, and joynes issue."[8] The "joyning of issue," with its obvious sexual implications, becomes a particularly common trope among the verse-writing lechers of seventeenth-century law satire. Ruggle's Ignoramus sets the style for much of the satire in this vein, especially in combining legal terminology with sexual innuendo. Ignoramus's lust for Rosabella relies heavily upon the language of the courts. On one occasion, for instance, while complaining that "Cupid would never leave me till he had caught me in his Bailywick," the lecherous old pettifogger describes the telling effect that his lust has had on his ability to concentrate. He is so obsessed that he can no longer perform his legal duties: "Now I am even as a fly without a head, I frisk and buz this way, and that way, and know not what I do; if I draw but a deed with a womans name in't. I presently write down Rosabella; for *corpus cum causa, corpus cum cauda*; for *noverint universi, amaverint universi*; for *habere ad rectum, habere ad lectum,* and so I spoile the whole deed" (1.2.52-62C). Together with the verbal play upon such legal phrases as "habeas corpus" and "joyne issue" which abound throughout the comedy, this speech reveals the lawyer's real motives in regard to the heroine. He wishes to attach her body, but not with cause but *cum cauda* (with tail). He wishes to bring her to trial, not in court but *ad lectum* (in bed). She will not become his wife, but his concubine.

Ignoramus's only reason for rejecting the heroine as a marital prospect is that she brings him no property. He hopes eventually to discard her in favor of a rich widow, some unfortunate creature with a fat jointure. When lawyers appear in seventeenth-century romantic comedy, they are usually in pursuit of rich young widows and heiresses, and most of these characters, like Ignoramus, are represented as old and often beyond the enjoyment of sexual love. Bartolus in Fletcher's *The Spanish Curate* is the typical *senex amans* whose jealousy makes him a hundred times more watchful of his young wife than the mythical Argus and whose greed and treachery make his enemies resolve to cuckold him. The unnamed lawyer in Fletcher's *A Wife for a Month* is ridiculed for his advances to a rich young widow. The lawyer, "trimm'd up like a galley foist," feels that he has a good matrimonial cause because he "can make her a jointure of any man's land in Naples; and she shall keep it too: I have a trick for it." He seems less eager to make her a jointure of his own lands. The fool Tony ascribes his motives solely to greed and suggests that the wife should be able to obtain a divorce because of the lawyer's sexual incapacity:

> He would look on her
> And read her over once a day, like a hard report,
> Feed his dull eye, and keep his fingers itching;
> For anything else she may appeal to a parliament:
> *Subpoenas* and *posteas* have spoiled his codpiece.[9]

During the Caroline period, we find far fewer references to legal lovers, a theme perhaps inappropriate to the more serious and politically based attacks of the Puritan moralists upon the lawyers. In Shirley's *Honoria and Mammon,* the wooing scenes between Lady Mammon and the lawyer Traverse have an obviously allegorical meaning. The emphasis is placed upon the theme of legal avarice. Nevertheless, the language vividly recalls the heyday of *Zepheria* and the *Gulling Sonnets* of Sir John Davies. The lawyer's motives for marriage are purely selfish; his main concern is to see himself seated on "the throne of Law," an achievement impossible without the lady's wealth. The wooing scene, unlike earlier versions of lovemaking in legalese, is based upon the language of the criminal rather than civil courts:

> *Traverse:*   I can court you
> In a more legal way, and in the name

Of love and law, arrest you, thus. (*Embraces her*)
Mammon: Arrest me?
Trav: And hold you fast, imprisoned in my arms,
Without bail or mainprise.
Mam: This does well.
Trav: I can do better yet, and put in such
A declaration, madam, as shall startle
Your merriest blood.
Mam: I may put in answer.
Trav: Then comes my replication, to which
You may rejoin.—*Currat lex!*
Shall we join issue presently?[10]

Later in the comedy, Traverse becomes infatuated with the lady Honoria, but he misunderstands the true nature of "honorable" love relationships, for he develops a scheme to marry Honoria while keeping Mammon as his concubine. He could not love Mammon half so much, loved he not Honoria more.

Most of these strains of anti-law satire are renewed in the Restoration period. Both Parkhurst and Ravenscroft retain Ignoramus's ludicrous love poetry in their Englishing of Ruggle's comedy for the popular stage.[11] The Latin is typical of satirized law jargon and simple enough to remain unchanged for the popular audience:

> *Si possem vellem pour te Rosa ponere pellem;*
> *Quicquid tu vis crava, & habebis singula brava:*
> *Et dabo* Fee-Simple, *si monstras* Love's pretty dimple,
> *Gownos, Silkcotos, Kirtellos, & Petticotos,*
> *Farthingalos, Biggos, Stomacheros, & Perriwiggos,*
> *Pantaflos, Cuffos, Garteros, Spanica-Ruffos,*
> *Buskos, & Soccos, Tifanos, & Cambrica-smockos,*
> *Pimpillos, Pursos: Ad ludos ibis & ursos,*
> *Anglice* Bear-Garden.[12]

In the original comedy, this poem reinforces the lawyer's continual emphasis upon things and his failure to understand spiritual values. In order to impress the heroine, he offers her material gifts and speaks of marriage as though it were a commercial transaction. The *ponere pellem* of the first line plays upon the term "*legum ponere*" or the "money down" for an object or service. Later in the same scene, Ignoramus offers Rosabella a marriage jointure, but we discover that the lawyer has so worked the document that it can be voided once he has achieved his sexual ambitions.[13] The lawyer's view of marriage, therefore, is uniform with his attitude toward the legal manipulation of real property.

As J. F. Gundy has indicated in his interesting but little-known study of Ruggle's play, the character of Hudibras is partly modeled upon that of Ignoramus.[14] Somewhat more quixotic and far less lecherous, the perambulating country justice of Butler's great burlesque poem is motivated more by a desire for financial security than by greed and lust in his amorous pursuit of the widow. Like all lawyer-lovers, Hudibras, J. P., is interested in the widow's jointure land, "for he in all his amorous battells, / No 'dvantage finds like goods and chattels." He also woos the widow in typical legalese, with his eye squarely on the main chance:

> Quoth he, if you'l joyn *Issue* on't,
> I'l give you satisfactory account;
> So you will promise, if you loose,
> To settle all, and be my Spouse.[15]

Like his ancestor Ignoramus, Hudibras fails in his marital expectations, receives a sound thrashing from the widow, and is also threatened with exorcism.

In the socially-oriented comedy of later seventeenth-century drama, the legal profession seems less prominently represented, so that lawyers appear mainly in subsidiary roles, as in the case of Congreve's Buckram in *Love for Love* or the many attorneys and barristers who crowd the stage in Wycherley's *The Plain Dealer*. Their customary role in these plays is to act as agents for those characters who have the power to destroy the happiness of romantic couples. Attorney Docket in *The Woman Turn'd Bully* is unusual in the sense that he combines these roles, first as Lucia's guardian and second as a greedy lawyer who wishes to profit from the marriage of his ward.[16] Many Restoration stage lawyers are actually earlier characters refashioned to meet contemporary dramatic needs. Attorney Bramble in Nahum Tate's *Cuckold's Haven* (1685) is based upon Mr. Bramble of Chapman and Jonson's *Eastward Hoe*; the toothless and palsied Bartoline in John Crowne's *The City Politiques* (1683) is a revised version of Fletcher's Bartolus in *The Spanish Curate*, a character further adapted into James Drake's *The Sham-Lawyer* (1691) as Serjeant-at-Law Wrangle. In these adaptations, the treatment of the lawyer-lover is somewhat more severe than in early Jacobean comedy, particularly in the fact that many actually become cuckolds and are submitted to much greater abuse at the hands (or tongues) of their mistresses. In *The Sham-Lawyer*, for example, the subplot from Fletcher's comedy is expanded and the legal characters more fully explored. The lawyer's wife Florella is not only considerably coarser than Fletcher's Amarintha but is also the former mistress of Careless, a typical Restoration rake much less moral and refined than Leandre. The activities of Wrangle and Affadavit (robbed of Fletcher's main plot concerning Don Henrique and Don Jamie) are more fully described, so that their knavery (even to the point of forging documents in disappearing ink) makes their humiliation all the more logical and deserved.

In the satire of this period, cuckoldom was the status most feared and most often achieved, so that it would not be surprising if lawyers played a prominent role in the romantic intrigues of rakes like Careless, albeit as victims rather than perpetrators. The most amusing treatment of this subject is Charles Gildon's "Session of Cuckolds" in his prose satire *Nuncius Infernalis* (1692).[17] In the trial scene, all the other professionals admit their culpability and offer only brief statements in justifications of themselves. Only the lawyers make a plea of not guilty. Their first concern is one of precedence since they have been forced to wait until many inferior tradesmen have had their say. They first plead that Lucifer's court is a court of equity and that since marriage is a form of suicide, their case should be removed into a criminal jurisdiction. Accepting the ruling of the court, however, they proceed to show that the bill has been incorrectly worded and that they should have a Writ of Error. At length, they do not deny that they are cuckolds but offer a "negative" proof to suggest that *"we did not get Mony to maintaine their Luxury, but they maintained their LUXURY out of the Mony that we got."* They are, one presumes, not so much cuckolds as cuckolded; their status is more passive than active. The devils all enjoy a hearty laugh, and the presiding judge has to intervene before the pleading lawyer can quite finish illustrating his point by reference to "another very pertinent *Precedent* in my Lord *Cook,* where *John a-Noake* is *Tenant* only for *Life,* and *John Astiles Tenant* in *Tail."* Predictably, old Nick decides that they shall be tenants in perpetuity in the depths below.[18]

In eighteenth-century satire, we find far less attention paid to legal lovemaking, poetic legalese, and cuckoldry. Ned Ward places a number of aged lawyer-cuckolds in his version of hell, and occasionally a lawyer pursues romantic interests, although rarely as a *professional* lover.[19] The chief fault charged to lawyers in Augustan satire is that they are either lechers or that they encourage prostitution for monetary gains. These accusations reach their peak in the first two decades of the century and gradually decline thereafter. Defoe seems particularly concerned about lawyers who promote the spread of bawdy houses, both for their own amusement and for personal profit. He is most strident in his criticism of the lascivious conduct of lawyers in high and responsible positions. In his *Reformation of Manners,* Defoe attacks a number of eminent lawyers like Lord Chancellor Sir William Cowper and Sir Salathiel Lovell, allowing full vent to his Calvinistic sense of moral outrage:

> Ride with the Judge and view the wrangling Bar,
> And see how lewd our *Justice-Merchants* are:
> How *Clito* comes from instigating Whore,
> Pleads for the Man he Cuckol'd just before;
> See how he Cants, and acts the Ghostly Father,
> And brings the Gospel and the Law together:

> To make his pious Frauds be well receiv'd,
> He quotes that Scripture which he ne're believ'd;
> Fluent in Language, indigent in Sence,
> Supplies his want of Law with Impudence.[20]

For these and similar attacks, Defoe was convicted of seditious libel and sentenced to the pillory, but he remains totally undaunted in his next assault upon the law in his *Hymn to the Pillory* (1704), repeating many of the same criticisms, if in somewhat more general terms:

> Let none such Bride-well Justices Protect,
> At first debauch the Whores which they Correct:
> Such who with Oaths and Drunk'ness sit,
> And Punish far less Crimes than they Commit.[21]

It appears that prostitution had become a serious social problem and that legal authorities were benefiting from the activities of bawds and prostitutes rather than cracking down on the offenders. Even *The Tatler* includes some guarded warnings about the sheer numbers of women involved in criminal cases of prostitution and rape, and it is even suggested that women be represented on juries. Mr. Spectator complains frequently about the looseness of lawyers' morals, as in the story of Lucinda Parley, a waitress at a coffeehouse who is courted by a lawyer. The young man neglects his career ("none come to him for Counsel but in *Forma Pauperis*") while he woos the young woman "at Discretion." According to his diary, the future chief justice, Dudley Ryder finds himself continually tempted by streetwalkers.[22] The fullest account of these problems is given in Swift's "Project for the Advancement of Religion," in which the irascible dean exposes the abuses of men in commission of the peace who actually enrich themselves to the debasement of society by encouraging vice on the streets. Apparently, it was the practice of some justices to exact protection money from all the bawds in their wards. These magistrates, as Swift ironically notes, cause twice as much vice since the women have to work much harder "to answer double Charges, of paying the Justice, and supporting themselves,"[23] Fielding's *The Coffee-House Politician* outlines the methods employed by justices in maintaining rigid control over the system by means of jurypacking. If a bawd is unwilling to submit to the justice's demand for payment, she will be arraigned before a jury of highly moral and responsible citizens. If she cooperates but must be brought to trial, the bawd or prostitute may look forward to a more favorable jury and, in any case, a lighter sentence.

During vacation time, when judges and their trains went on circuit to the assize towns, the lawyers did not scruple, we are told, to introduce their vice and depravity into the provinces. A broadside ballad, attributed to Swift, describes such occasions, according to the title, as "Helter Skelter." Gaily attired in borrowed clothing, pettifoggers invade the countryside, "thorough Town and thorough Village, / All to plunder, all to pillage."[24] In addition to stirring up all manner of civil strife, the lawyers devote much ingenuity to the sport of cuckolding local farmers and to tumbling the country wenches. One ironist suggests that, in order to arrest this new disease plaguing the countryside, the chancellor and the senior judges should introduce a set of rules regarding circuit work, one of which would stipulate "that no *Serjeant* or *Counsellor* shall be suffered to go, that is *under* FIFTY, unless he will agree to defray out of his *Briefs,* the charges of a *Chaplain's* attendance to give him *Spiritual* Admonition and *ghostly* Counsel against having *two* FLESH Suppers the same night." The general view of legal lechery in this period may be summed up in the following piece of wit entitled "To Serjeant D__, Lincoln's Inn, an old Practitioner":

> I'm for no Prudes so prim and queasy:
> Give *Me* a Girl that's *free* and *easy,*
> Quoth Serjeant D__, nor do I fear
> My fame or money here or there;
> For 'tis the d__l to be catch'd!
> When once by *Husband* You are watch'd'
> Besides a thousand other ills
> As Witness late Chief Justice W__[25]

The impression one receives from eighteenth-century satire is that lawyers are usually the predators, active rather than passive, while their wooing is inspired not only by lust but also by greed. In *Law Is a Bottomless Pit,* attorney Hocus's interest in John Bull's wife is predicated upon such dual motives. She is not only an easy sexual conquest but also the best avenue in the lawyer's pursuit of mercenary ambitions in regard to the lucrative suit between Bull and Baboon. Fielding's works are filled with bawdy and grasping lawyers and justices whose lust is only tempered by financial opportunism. Squeezum in *The Coffee-House Politician* takes bribes and protection money from bawds, but his lecherous resolve to "keep" the heroine leads to his inevitable ruin. The much sought-after widow in his *Love in Several Masques* condemns the manner of legal courting as self-seeking and demeaning. The lawyer approaches her as one "who attacks me as he would a jury, with a cringe, and a lie at the tip of his tongue" (2.1). At the worst, lawyer-lovers are out-and-out blackguards like Murphy in Fielding's *Amelia,* whose complicity with the heroine's sister cheats Amelia of her rightful inheritance and brings misery and degradation upon the cheated mistress. Murphy's treachery is eventually exposed only by the deathbed confession of one of the witnesses to the forged will, and the lawyer is finally caught, tried, and hanged for his crimes. In most cases, however, the lawyer appears as a comic rather than a serious victim of his lust, as in the amusing story of *The Lawyer and Nell,* where the lawyer successfully engineers the seduction of Nell by making false and extravagant promises.[26] He wins the first phase of the love contest by getting her pregnant with no intention of remaining true, even though he has solemnly sworn to Old Nick that he would abide by his promises. When, however, he jilts her in order to take up with a new mistress, Nell and her friend the chimney sweep dress up as devils and put the fear of Old Nick into the lawyer. Using firecrackers and gunpowder, the two devils in disguise scare the lawyer into marrying Nell as he had sworn, thus achieving an equitable solution to Nell's unwed motherhood.

In most of these stories, the lawyer occupies a role which in earlier literature had been filled by monks, friars, usurers, and the diabolical Jesuits. In the fabliaux of the Middle Ages, the legal profession plays virtually no part in the world's condemnation of lust and prostitution; but, as each of the old satirical targets disappears from the English scene, the lawyer inherits the conventional roles of bawdy literature: the deceiver deceived, the *senex amans* vexed in love and marriage, and the deserving cuckold. During the sixteenth and seventeenth centuries, these satirical conventions remain relatively generalized and are employed in attacking vices which are typical of all humanity. In the more particularized satire of the late seventeenth and eighteenth centuries, the lawyer plays only an incidental role in the treatment of love and lechery, and the principal criticism stresses such real problems as prostitution promoted by the lesser officials of the law but inadequately controlled by the senior ranks of the profession. Apart from the specific issues, the literary satire of lawyer-lovers confines its attention to a few less principled individuals such as any age produces. Thus, the love conventions discussed in this chapter are usually accretions to, rather than the central elements of, the lawyer's literary representation.

Ignoramus Lawyers

Excepting his incidental alignment with the vice figures, whose conduct is noticeably ridiculous and unlearned, the literary lawyer of the Middle Ages is not typically characterized as foolish and ignorant. Occasionally in the fabliaux one might find such a lawyer, as in the French farce *Maitre Pathélin,* but such characters are rare. In the main, the lawyer of medieval literature, like Chaucer's Man of Law, is knowledgeable and competent. He may be cruel, avaricious, and hypocritical, but he is invariably skilled in the practice of his profession. If he was ignorant, it was only in the moral sense, for he had failed to head the divine mandate to employ his superior intellect in the spirit of *charitas.* In *Mundus et Infans* (c. 1500), the lawyer's name is Folye, but there is a world of difference between this character's ignorance and mere stupidity because he is apparently astute enough to be a king's serjeant and to gull the uplanders. In another famous morality play, *Hyckescorner* (c.1530), the legal profession is associated with the vice Imagynacion who claims that lawyers would be lost without his assistance and inspiration. It is Imagynacion who enables them to "prove right wrong, and all by reason."[27] The vice's claim may be entirely lost upon the modern reader who believes that "imagination" is a pedagogical virtue, but in its older sense, imagination was the lowest faculty upon the scale of knowing, often equated with illusion and false dreams, the darker and distorted images of higher reality. Thus, the "reason" used by Imagynacion's lawyers could only be diabolically inspired. It is primarily in this sense of "folly" that we must classify the ignorance of medieval representations of lawyers.

The term "ignoramus" had no derogatory connotations during the Middle Ages. From the Latin "do not know," it was the legal term used in grand jury proceedings for not finding indictments because of insufficient evidence. It was the counterpart of the term *"billa vera"* (true bill) which determined that an indictment be brought before the petit jury. According to the *OED,* the earliest use of "ignoramus" in its general modern sense (referring to any stupid individual) occurs in Beaumont and Fletcher's *The Honest Man's Fortune* (1613) in the rhetorical question "Wouldst thou come / To point of marriage with an ignoramus?" In this passage, however, the authors probably intended a legal sense of the term, for the speaker's opinion reflects the widely accepted view that one should not venture into marriage without the evidence to justify the decision, without which it is difficult to say whether the intended spouse is the true bill of goods. In any case, a clearer use of the word in its general sense appears in Nimble's question to Tresilian concerning the signing of the blank charters in *Woodstock* (1584): "But how if we meet with some ignoramus fellows, my lord, that cannot write their mind: what shall they do?" (3.1) Even though the play deals with legal subjects and Nimble is a law clerk, the use of the term in this passage clearly refers to ignorance per se, and the general sense of the word is further reinforced by the fact that Master Ignorance, Bailiff of Dunstable, has an illiterate brother named Ignoramus.

The popularization of the term "ignoramus," however, is largely due to the success of Ruggle's Latin comedy *Ignoramus,* not to mention the numerous ballads and satirical responses the comedy inspired. One must also remark the comedy's continuing influence in provoking apologetic replies years after its first performance. As late as 1648, some thirty-five years after the initial triumph at Cambridge, Serjeant Robert Callis, who had been a student at Gray's Inn during the great struggle between Coke and James I, published *The Case and Argument against Sir Ignoramus of Cambridge.*[28] Probably written in 1617, this work has little to recommend it, as a satirical response to Ruggle's work, except that it illustrates the continuing currency of the anti-law satire. In later years, the term "ignoramus" becomes almost synonymous with legal abuses, particularly those of bribing, packing, and intimidating juries. After the Middlesex grand jury's rejection of a bill against the Earl of Shaftesbury in 1681, we notice an increase in the use of "ignoramus" in reference to grand jury proceedings. Chief Justice John Vaughan's *Ignoramus Vindicated, In a Dialogue between Prejudice and Indifference* (1681) concerns "that sort of Folks called *Ignoramus-men*, that refuse some times to find *Bills*, though there be *Positive Oaths* before them."[29] According to this eminent lawyer, the fault is not in the system but in those who are called upon to make it work and who do not live up to their responsibilities as English citizens. From a different angle, Edward Whitaker's *The Ignoramus Justices* (1681) mirrors Vaughan's general concern but places greater blame upon the authorities who have the power to counteract indifference and who have the responsibility to prevent injustices.[30] The morally oriented pamphlet attacks a series of verdicts given at the Middlesex assizes in which the terms of the statutes against Catholic recusants had been applied to dissenting Protestants. The justices were exceeding their statutory powers by misconstruing the intent of existing legislation. An anonymous broadside entitle "Ignoramus: An Excellent New Song" (1681) satirizes the same problem from the Tory point of view:

> Since Reformation,
>   With *Whig's* in Fashion,
> There's neither Equity nor Justice in the Nation.
>   Against their Furies,
>   There no Cure is,
> As lately hath been wrought by *Ignoramus-Juries*.[31]

One reason for the continuing popularity of the term "ignoramus" during the Restoration was the revival of interest in the play itself, which had been the delight of Charles's "Royall Grandfather of blessed memory." No fewer than three authors sought royal recognition by translating *Ignoramus* into English: Ferdinando Parkhurst (c.1660), Robert Codrington (1662), and Edward Ravenscroft (1678).[32] Codrington's work is an accurate word-for-word rendering of Ruggle's original based on the 1658 edition of the Latin play, but this version was not intended for the stage. Parkhurst's *Ignoramus* was performed both at Drury Lane and at Whitehall. Ravenscroft's *The English Lawyer* was also performed several times upon the London stage and was revived as late as 1736 under the old title of *Ignoramus*. The Latin play went through a remarkable total of thirteen editions from 1630 to 1787. During the eighteenth century, the Latin *Ignoramus* became almost standard fare at Westminster School.[33] Thus, it would be easy to underestimate the importance of Ruggle's original Latin work in the development of anti-law satire.

The plot of *Ignoramus* is typical of comedy in the Italian vein, with its stock characters: the wily servant, identical twins, the *leno, senex amans,* and *parasitus.*[34] Apart from the strong influence of the morality tradition upon the characterization of the lawyer, the new ignoramus type also combines the Latin *advocatus* and the pedant, as they are introduced into English literature through the Italian *commedia erudita.* Although based immediately upon Della Porta's *La Trappolaria* (1596), Ruggle's comedy reveals throughout the author's familiarity with Roman drama, not only from the *Pseudolis* of Plautus but also in several conventions not used in *La Trappolaria.* The ludicrous pedantry of Ruggle's comic lawyer may also owe something to the Latin *Pedantius* (c. 1581), particularly in its satire of inflated law language.[35] The Cambridge author may also have been familiar with the pedants of the popular stage, such as the one in Shakespeare's *The Taming of the Shrew* or Holofernes in *Love's Labour's Lost,* the schoolmaster hanged for his "patientia" and equivocal verses in *Woodstock,* or Gerrold "by title paedogogus" in Shakespeare and Fletcher's *The Two Noble Kinsmen.* The last example, from a comedy written only two years before Ruggle's, is more interesting because the jailer's daughter actually takes Gerrold to be a conjurer and asks him to raise a devil.

For our purposes, the real significance of *Ignoramus* is that it so successfully amalgamates all the various representations of law satire. Ignoramus is an ambidextrous vice, a lecher, a comical Zepherian poet, an enemy to civil peace, and, of course, the quintessential ignoramus. As Musaeus, his academic clerk, wryly observes, Ignoramus's mother was called Barbara Latina, for indeed the play is filled with the kind of mutilated Latin that humanistic critics of the law so heartily deplored. With the revival of the classics in the early sixteenth century, it was inevitable that medieval Law Latin and French should come under fire from university scholars. Sir Thomas Elyot, educated at Oxford and the Middle Temple, insists in *The Book Named the Governour* (1531) that classical literature and rhetoric be made a prerequisite to the study of law. He also expresses his distaste for the crudities of common law language: "Also that reverend study is involved in so barbarous a language, that it is not only void of all eloquence, but also being separate from the exercise of our law only, it serveth no commodity or necessary purpose, no man understanding it but they which have studied the laws."[36] For these reasons, Elyot suggests a program of "the right study of very philosophy" for aspiring lawyers until, at the age of twenty-one, they are "set to the laws of this realm (being once brought to a more certain and compendious study, and either in English, Latin, or good French, written in a more clean and elegant style) ..." (1,xiv). In an unpublished tract, *A Persuasion to the King,* Richard Morison also strongly promotes the study of the classics and recommends that all English laws be written in good Latin, ascribing much of the confusion and uncertainty of the common law to its great jumble of languages:

> And where the comen lawes ... be not certeyn, and the bokes that concerne the same
> be nowe written in no parfit tonge, but myngled with dyvers languages, som words

saxon, som britishe, som Italian, some Latyn, some frennshe, som englisshe, yea and some greke, and som noon of all these, it is very expediant, and as I thynke very necessarye that they wer reduced to som one parfet tonge. For the dyversite of tonges bredeth moche confusion and causeth many doutes and questions to growe of the etymologye and interpretation of wordes.[37]

Because of these linguistic difficulties, Morison complains, there are many lawyers who are incapable of drafting deeds and pleadings and who actually begin this work in Law French, leaving it to their clerks to translate the documents into Latin. Yet, as if this problem were not enough, there were also certain men in the profession who frowned upon and discouraged the study of the Latin classics, who "when they perceyve any yong man geven to goode learnyng, desirous therwyth to have the knowlage of the lawes, they will utterly dissuade them to forgett and leve his old studie, as thoughe good lettres and the lawe coulde not agree in one person."[38] This tendency is demonstrated in Ignoramus's open contempt for his "universitans" Musaeus and the study of the seven liberal arts.

During the Tudor period, many authorities seem to feel that this grievous state of affairs was exacerbated by the great influx of lower class individuals into the profession. The general belief was that the law was no longer the sole domain of gentlemen and that too many lawyers were coming to the Inns of Court with inadequate educational preparation.[39] According to some critics, like Abraham Fraunce, these new lawyers had no respect for rhetoric, logic, and the purity of the Latin tongue. They were *rabulae forensis*, "who, when their fathers have made some lewd bargain in the country, run immediately to the Inns of Court, and having in seven years space met with six French words, home they ride again like brave Magnificos, and dash their poor neighbors children quite out of countenance, with villen in gros, villen regardant, and Tenant per le curtesie. . . ."[40]

To some extent, Tudor and Jacobean lawyers may have used their terms of art deliberately to intimidate and confuse their clients and enemies. Lincus in Daniel's *The Queene's Arcadia* employs such tactics in his fruitless campaign against the Arcadians. As he explains to Alcon:

> I overwhelme
> My practise too, with darkness, and strange words;
> With paragraphs, Conditions, Codicilles,
> Acceptilations, actions, recissorie,
> Noxall and Hypotheticall, and involve
> Domestike matter in a forraine phrase.
>
> (lines 1088-93)

The foreign phrasing in this quotation refers to categories of civil rather than common law. Scores of stage lawyers pursue the same basic strategy in contemporary drama, notably those like Ignoramus, Practice, Sanitonella, Bartolus, Pety-fog, and Dodge (*Cure for a Cuckold*). In a lighter vein, Davies employs such legal obscurities in routing the insufferable Gallas, who has been parading his newly acquired technical vocabulary from the field of military engineering:

> But, to require such gulling tearmes as these,
> With words of my profession, I reply;
> I tell of fourching, vouchers, and counterpleas,
> Of withernams, essoynes, and Champerty.
>   So neither of us understanding one another,
>   We part as wise as when we came together.[41]

The main stress of the second line falls nicely upon "my," suggesting the ease with which the lawyer puts his rival to flight. Ignoramus experiences supreme delight in using such obsolete terms as *sac, soc, tol, tem, infangtheof,* and *outfangtheof,* words which may have been located in such specialized dictionaries as Rastell's *Termes de la ley,* West's *Symboleography,* or Cowell's *Interpreter.* Such terms would not have troubled most lawyers, of course, but they must have sounded strange to the uninitiated. According to another stage lawyer, who claims to have studied the common law for twenty-three years, the preoccupation with such recondite words stems from an inbred melancholy:

> 'Tis food to some,
> My lord. There are old men at the present
> That are so poison'd with th' affectation
> Of law-words, having had many suits canvass'd,
> That their common talk is nothing but barb'rous
> Latin: they cannot so much as pray, but
> In law, that their sins may be remov'd, with
> A writ of error, and their souls fetch'd up
> To heaven with a *certiorari.*[42]

The belief that a liberal use of technical terms seals and verifies one's intellectual brilliance is a common enough failing. Even today, when such pretensions ought to be less tolerated, every field has its own peculiar jargon and its own myopic preoccupations. If the height of one's expectations is to impress the provincials, then a superficial knowledge of a subject seems innocuous, even amusing. The situation alters for the worse, however, when superficiality of learning threatens to engulf a discipline, as for example when twenty precedents will make a case, or when all reality must be translated into statistics, or when rather pedestrian thinking parades under the title of hermeneutics, or when so-called scholars write whole chapters in the passive voice. It is this kind of nagging, irritating sub-intellect which, if projected back into Tudor-Stuart times, provoked learned authors into their stinging condemnation of ignoramuses. However, we must not suppose that the satirists even as much as dreamed of including the eminent and learned lawyers within the arc of their raillery. As we have seen, it was chiefly the lawyers, or literary artists with Inns of Court backgrounds, who led the assault against bad Latin, lack of education, and against those individuals who neglected their studies at the Inns.

If we may trust the character sketches written by men like Overbury, Lenton, Earle, and Saltonstall, we can piece together an alarming picture of legal learning. "The young barrester," says Lenton, "is one call'd too't by Reading, though he never read for't, and hath tane his leave of *Littleton* before he was wel acquainted with him." As a student, the young barrister has squandered his time wenching instead of attending moots, studying "poetry instead of Perkins," He is likely to "break his head" if confronted with a difficult problem in logic, or as Overbury puts it, he thinks no language worth studying and "he hath bene a long time at warres with Priscian."[43] Webster's Inns-a-Court man is best remembered for his arrogance and bad Latin: "He will talk ends of *Latin,* though it be false, with as great confidence, as ever *Cicero* could pronounce on Oration, though his best authors for't, be Tavernes and Ordinaries.... You shall never see him melancholie, but when he wants a newe Suite, or feares a Sergant: At which times onely, hee betakes himselfe to *Ployden.* By that he hath reade *Littleton,* he can call *Solon, Lycurgus,* and *Justinian,* fooles, and dares compare his Law to a *Lord Cheife-Justices.*"[44]

The lower ranks of attorneys, solicitors, and clerks fare no better. Earle's Attorney "ha's some smatch of a Scholler, and yet uses Latin very hardly, and lest it should accuse him, cuts it off in the midst and will not let it speake out." Most of these practitioners began as clerks "of a swooping *Dash,*" who could "chatter out some tearmes of Law, with more audacity than knowledge," but who "for feare of writing false Latin, abbreviates the ending and termination of his word with a dash, and so leaves it doubtfull."[45] In most of these characters, the representation of the ignoramus is underscored by the authors' reverence for classical education, the great legal authorities like Plowden, Perkins, and Littleton, and for the senior members of the profession.

The worst faults are combined and magnified in the seminal figure of Ignoramus. To borrow Serjeant Maynard's phrase, Ignoramus was a walking *ars bablativa,* who confounds himself rather than his adversaries. Though he is aware of the necessity of correct grammar in legal documents and even claims to have won cases by finding verbal and grammatical inaccuracies, he is not confident about his own or his clerk's ability to draft instruments in correct Latin. On one occasion, instead of correcting Dulman's Latin, he recommends the use of abbreviations and dashes: "If thou canst not write true Latin, thou mayst *scribere cum dasho,* that is cut off thy words in the middle, with quirks and dashes, as Lawyers do, so thou shalt neither erre in Latin nor in the law" (4.7.7-11C).

Since Latin is an inflected language, it is easy to see why those lawyers and scholars concerned about the purity of language took exception to this practice. Throughout the seventeenth century, the feeling prevails that certain lawyers were more interested in the formulaic accuracy of legal writing than in either the intellectual integrity of the language or the true meaning and intent of words. Musaeus's opinion that there is not "soe great an enemy to knowledge / As Ignoramus. 'Tis he, and such as hee, / That overthrows all lawful government" (2.6.39-41B) is not less severe than the views expressed in the works of many other contemporary satirists of the law. Marston, himself a member of the Middle Temple, stigmatizes legal language as a confusion of tongues, "the barbarous blacksaunt of the Geat." Butler's criticism of legal language is particularly biting, as in the *ars bablativa* of Hudibras and his representation of the common lawyer who "overruns *Latin* and *French* with greater Barbarism, than the *Goths* did *Italy* and *France,* and makes as mad a Confusion of Language by mixing both with English."[46] The periodical comparison of legal language with the biblical account of the confusion of tongues at the Tower of Babel suggests that linguistic ignorance actually stems from the diabolical ambition of lawyers. To the humanistic critic of the law, the greatest single obstacle to the establishment of truth and justice is the failure of communication. In the opinion of men like Butler, lawyers are guilty not only of adulterating language but also of confusing meaning for their own selfish purposes:

> Others believe no *Voice* t' an *Organ*;
> So sweet as *Lawyers* in his *Bar-gown.*
> Until, with subtle Cobweb-Cheats,
> Th' are catch'd in knotted *Law,* like *Nets*:
> In which when once they are imbrangled,
> The more they stir the more th' are tangled,
> And while their *Purses* can dispute,
> There's no end of th' immortal Suit.[47]
> (2.3.15-22)

Other later Restoration writers were not slow to attack this kind of legal ignorance and dishonesty, as they saw it. The lawyer Quaint in Wycherley's *The Plain Dealer* makes a typical statement of the ways in which he misuses language and the skills of argumentation:

I will, as I see cause, extenuate, or exemplifie Matter of Fact; baffle Truth, with Impudence; answer Exceptions, with Questions, tho' never so impertinent; for Reasons, give 'em Words; for Law and Equity, Tropes and Figures: And so relax and enervate the sinews of their Argument, with the oyl of my Eloquence.... With

poignant and sowre Invectives, I say, I will deface, wipe out, and obliterate his fair
Reputation, even as a Record with the juice of Lemons; and tell such a Story, (for, the
truth on't is, all that we can do for our Client in *Chancery,* is telling a Story) a fine
Story, a long Story, such a Story—
(3.1.164-79)

Quaint is not in the least dismayed that the poet whose reputation he plans to
obliterate has been slandered by his client Manly for having the intelligence of a
lawyer. For money, Wycherley's lawyers will do anything, even support a slur
against their own professional dignity. In the socially oriented comedy of the
Restoration and Augustan periods, the legal profession fell to its nadir in popular
and literary esteem. The ridicule of legal language in the ignoramus tradition was
kept alive in the numerous minor legal characters that populate the late
seventeenth-century stage, as even the names testify: Quaint, Blackacre, Jolt,
Bartoline, Bramble, Buckram, Wrangle, Affidavit, and Puzzle, to list a few.

The clearest example of the direct influence of Ruggle's *Ignoramus* occurs in
the anonymous comedy *A Woman Turn'd Bully* (1675) in the figures of Attorney
Docket and his two clerks Dashwel and Spruce.[48] The main plot bears a number
of close resemblances to that of *Ignoramus* except that Docket is the guardian of
rather than the suitor to the heroine, Lucia. Docket, like the *leno* Torcol, is
actuated by greed and desires only to make money out of the marriage of his ward.
The threat to the heroine's happiness stems from the terms of her father's will
which stipulates that she can only obtain her inheritance of six thousand pounds
if she marries with her uncle Docket's consent. Failing this Docket will receive
the money, and, thus, it is the attorney's avarice which sets off the complicated
tricks which ultimately result in his being forced to acquiesce in Lucia's choice.
Just as Ignoramus accepts the wrong lover in the Polla-Rosabella swap, Docket
makes a similar mistake, although he actually marries his own maid-servant
instead of the Widow Goodfeild, whose goods and chattels he deems a suitable
compensation for the loss of Lucia's inheritance. Much of the law satire aimed at
Ignoramus and his clerks is reiterated in the relationship between old Docket,
Dashwel, and Spruce. Docket is represented as "a pure downright Attorney, with
as little mixture of Gentleman or Scholar as possible can be imagined" (B2v), and
his notion of a sound education may be gauged from his plans for his niece: "And
for Education, you shall have enough, *Lucy.* I scorn it should be said that any of my
Bloud should want Education. Dashwel shall teach ye French, he understands
Littleton perfectly well: And if you please, I'll have a Master come and teach ye to
cast Account, and write Short-hand" (C2r). Dashwel the "puny" clerk is the real
Ignoramus of the comedy in linguistic terms, for he is "so full of his Law-terms,
he can't speak without 'em" (B1v), and he betrays his true genealogy with his
first appearance upon stage when he makes the reply, "To that, Sir, I answer
Ignoramus. I can say little" (B2r). Goodfeild pokes rather pointed fun at him by
asking him a question lifted directly from *Ignoramus*: "Pray, Sir, *quota cloka?*"[49]

Dashwel understands, as the modern reader may not, that Goodfeild wants to know the time. A number of other verbal echoes occur between the two plays, such as the unusual phrase *"super naculum"* which is employed in a scene where several characters conspire to get Docket drunk, just as Trico and Cupes encourage Dulman to drink to excess in the similar scene from *Ignoramus* (3.2).

Close cousin to Docket is the country attorney Latitat in Grimston's *Lawyer's Fortune* (1705), a comedy which demonstrates the continuing vitality of the ignoramus tradition in the early eighteenth century.[50] The lawyer's name is based upon the writ of *latitat* ("he lurks in hiding"), the famous judicial writ of arrest issuing out of King's Bench in civil suits. The attorney is a notorious "knave in grain" who uses legal terminology to impress or bamboozle his clients. Having "as much Impudence, and as little Understanding as a Horse-racer; no more Honour than a Scotch Lord, no more Honesty than a French Taylor, and no more Religion than an English whore or a canting Informer" (C1r), Latitat hatches schemes which threaten to subvert the harmony of rural life in the community in which he "lurks." His career comes to a humiliating end when his victims discover the extent of the attorney's treachery and engineer a counterplot to recover their losses. Like most ignoramuses, Latitat overestimates his powers of cunning and extends his operations into intelligent society.

In the preface to *The Funeral* (1702), Richard Steele describes law as "an Art to be learn't to Speak our own Sense in other Men's words," a kind of *"Hocus Pocus,* that without you can repeat such and such words, you cannot convey what is in your hands into another's." In the play itself, the author exemplifies this view of the law in the character of Counsellor Puzzle, "eloquent in Gibberish," who flagrantly abuses the trust of his client Lord Brumpton. At the beginning of the play, the laywer calls upon the widow, Lady Brumpton, concerning her husband's will, and, while she pretends to compose herself, Puzzle and his clerk are left in the waiting-room alone. Little do they suspect that Lord Brumpton is not dead but actually listening from behind a curtain to everything they say. Puzzle seizes the opportunity to instruct his clerk on the fine art of his trade. He explains that he has cheated his old client by making "his whole Estate liable to an Hundred *per* Annum" for himself, on the premise that "a True Lawyer never makes any man's Will but his own." Then he has the clerk read a portion of the will in order to demonstrate the art of legal tautology, which he upholds as the first, second, and third excellence of legal language: "let others Think of logick, Rhetorick and I know not what impertinence but mind thou Tautology." He expresses the firm hope that he will see the day "when the Indenture shall be the exact measure of the Land that passes by it." The lawyer is interrupted in his reading of the parchment but not before he has given the audience a sample of his tautologies in such typical Latin as "Ego Predict, Comes de Brumpton—*Totas meas Barnos—Outhousas, & Stabulas—Yardos,* etc."[51] The Law Latin of the stage becomes even more ludicrous with each new version of it.

Perhaps the most concerted and acerbic attacks upon legal ignorance and duplicity appear in the works of the Scriblerians Swift, Pope, Arbuthnot, and Gay. One of the earliest pieces is the pamphlet series collected under the title of *Law Is a Bottomless Pit* (1712) by Dr. John Arbuthnot. The forerunner to *John Bull,* this prose satire features the ludicrous figure of Humphrey Hocus, an "old cunning Attorney, what he wanted of Law, was made up by a Clerk which he kept."[52] The main plot of *Bottomless Pit* involves the Bull family in a lawsuit arising from Philip Baboon's forcible entry upon the estate of Lord Strutt by dint of a forged will. The attorney manages to prolong the suit for more than ten years by hiring witnesses and bribing juries, all the while fleecing John Bull by the accumulation of his own fees. In desperation, John at one point resolves to become an ignoramus himself by spouting the babble of law terms in his own defense, but to no avail.[53] Hocus even suggests that John has become maddened by the law, and he calls in Don Diego the conjurer to assist him in bringing John back to his senses. It is not madness which leads John into financial peril so much as his typically British stubbornness. He might easily have averted the disastrous consequences of the suit had he simply dropped it upon the first demurrer, or at least had he hired an honest attorney.

Among the Augustan wits, Swift was certainly the most persistent critic of the legal profession, and clearly the most famous piece of anti-law invective in the whole of English literature is Gulliver's devastating account of the profession to the Master Houyhnhnm. In this attack upon legal corruption, lawyers are said to be "a society of men among us bred from their youth in the art of proving by words multiplied for the purpose, that white is black and black is white, according as they are paid." Ignoring the poor and feeding upon the rich, lawyers are guilty of padding fees, bribing judges, encouraging "fraud, perjury, and oppression," deliberately disguising their iniquities under a "peculiar cant and jargon of their own" and by recording, under the title of precedents, "all the decisions formerly made against common justice and the general reason of mankind." For these and other reasons, lawyers are therefore judged "the most ignorant and stupid generation among us, the most despicable in common conversation, avowed enemies to all knowledge and learning, and equally disposed to pervert the general reason of mankind in every other subject of discussion as in their own profession."[54] While this remarkable diatribe bears much in common with the humanistic criticism of earlier authors like Erasmus, More, and Montaigne, it is clearly different in tone. It is much closer to the diatribe delivered by Musaeus in *Ignoramus,* but we must remember that Musaeus confined his remarks to pettifoggers. Swift's works rarely make such distinctions. Lacking the detachment and the discrimination of earlier satire, this passage betrays the impatience of a man whose disapprobation stems from real rather than imaginary causes. In his public life, Swift seemed always in conflict with the lawyers. His *Drapier Letters* are filled with scathing remarks about the legal profession and the administration of the common law in Ireland. However, in spite of his stated preference for generalized satire, Swift (like Defoe) in his own works launches several attacks upon particular individuals, such as Serjeant Bettesworth (King's Second Serjeant in Ireland) and William Whitshed (Lord Chief Justice of Ireland).[55] Fortunately, the myth of Swift's lifelong melancholia has now been largely dispelled, so that we can safely say that his dislike for his real adversaries colored his entire view of the profession.[56]

Swift's satire often reflects the current realities and problems of the legal world, as chapter 2 reveals. We have already seen enough to convince even the most sympathetic reader of the poverty of legal education during the Augustan period. The dean's apparent dislike of precedents parallels the contemporary hardening of the doctrine of binding precedent (stare decisis), a development which threatened to hinder the judge's application of reason and logic in individual cases.[57] Even so mild-mannered a man as John Evelyn believed that lawyers spent too much time studying archaic and insular English law when they might derive greater benefit from a classical education, particularly in the moral philosophy of Cicero and Seneca.[58] Although it may well be granted that Swiftian satire is characterized by a pungency and acerbity all its own, we must also recognize that Swift's view of the legal world often reflects a general lack of faith typical of most anti-law criticism of the Augustan age, regardless of the political, religious, and professional affiliations of the writers concerned.

Swift was not alone in ascribing the barbarity of legal language to ignorance and willfull obscurantism. The anonymous author of *Pettifoggers* (1723) compares lawyers to Romish priests who "preach up Religion, who have none, / By keeping others Ignorant, / By Arts abstruse and learned Cant."[59] Wherever they appear, lawyers are invariably satirized for their verbosity, tautologies, and affected eloquence. Even the lawyer-author Henry Fielding liberally sprinkles his works with ignoramuses of this kind, such as Mr. Brief in *Don Quixote in England,* who when he has received a good drubbing from the fiery old idealist, complains, "O, Sir Thomas! I am abused, beaten, hurt, maimed, disfigured, defaced, dismembered, killed, massacred, and murdered by this rogue, robber, rascal, villain" (3.15). With great peril, he persists in having his action of battery. In *The Champion,* responding to the query whether an action lies if a man describes an author as dull, Mr. Counsellor Vinegar renders his opinion in Law French:

Moy semble quod si ascun dit de J. S. eteant un poete quod est dull. Action bien voit gyser et le resolution de le case, I. R. A. 55S. 16. *Bien agree ove ceo ubi action fuit port per un apprentice del ley et plt declare quod deft avoit dit de luy quod est dunce,* and will get nothing by the law. *Et le opinion del court, fuit quod bien gist, car home poet estre heavie et nemy tam pregnant come ascuns auters sont et* encore un bon lawyer. *Mes quia il avoit dit que il ne voet get ascun chose per la ley. Action gist. Sic icy car si poete soit heavie ou dull non voit gett ascun chose* en le world.[60]

At this time, Fielding must have been struggling through the old Law French texts (such as Rolle's *Abridgement* here cited by the Champion), and certainly none but a lawyer, well acquainted with the idiosyncrasies of law language, could have produced such a felicitous blend of Latin, Old French, and English, with its accurate yet planned exaggeration: the typical phraseology, the total lack of intelligible punctuation, the frequent abbreviations, and the complete disregard of the normal inflections of Latin and French.[61] It would be useless to attempt a direct translation of the passage, but since it is necessary for the modern reader, I offer the following:

> It seems to me that if anyone says of J. S. being a poet that he is dull, an action may well lie, and the resolution of the case in Rolle's *Abridgement,* Volume 1, page 55, section 16 agrees well with the objection which was brought by an apprentice of the law where the plaintiff declared that the defendant had said of him that he is a dunce and will earn nothing by the law. And the opinion of the court was that an action well lies because one can be dense and not so filled with knowledge as other people are and still be a good lawyer. But because he said that he will earn nothing by the law, the action lies. So in this case, if the poet is stupid or dull, he will not get anything in the world.

Even with the translation, the logic of the opinion may seem far from clear, but according to the law of actionable words, Counsellor Vinegar is merely suggesting that, although the words "dull" and "stupid" are not actionable per se, an action lies if the words contain an implication of incompetence in the conduct of one's trade or profession, so that one's business is impaired by the slander. Thus, in this case, presumably, the action lies because the poet will not be able to earn a living. The main point of Fielding's use of Rolle is to emphasize the possibility that one can be dull and stupid and yet earn a living practicing law.

The funniest spoof of legalese, which anticipates some of the best of A. P. Herbert's *Misleading Cases,* is the remarkable case of *Stradling v. Styles,* an anonymous contribution to the reports of Scriblerus, and a piece which has been attributed to Sir William Fortescue, Master of the Rolls and close friend of Alexander Pope.[62] Based upon standard law reports going back to the sixteenth century, in black-letter Law French, *Stradling v. Styles,* contains all the typical ingredients together with excellent satire of formal pleading by opposing counsel. The dispute concerns a will in which the phraseology creates a ridiculous ambiguity, sufficiently intriguing it appears to occupy the attention of "touts les Justices" of the Court of Common Pleas: "*Le Report del Case argue en le commen Banke devants touts les Justices de mesme le Banke, en le quart an du raygne de Roy* Jacques, *entre* Matthew Stradling, *Plant. et* Peter Styles, *Def. en un Action propter certos Equos coloratos, Anglice,* Pyed Horses, *port per le dit* Matthew *vers le dit* Peter." The dispute arises from the will of Sir John Swale who has devised to Matthew *all* his black and white horses, but since Sir John had owned six black, six white, and six pied horses, *le dit* Peter has taken possession of the latter because they are neither all black nor all white. Matthew claims them because they are black-and-white. The pleading is marked by long winded digressions into Bracton, Littleton, and various archaic statutes, by considerable discussion concerning the substantial and formal nature of horses, and eventually by an issue joined over the term *coloratos*. Like the Champion's case of the dull poet, this brilliant tour-de-force could only have been written by someone, like Fortescue, deeply versed in legal history. Although the whole case is manifestly ridiculous, it is nevertheless couched in language so closely related to actual legal reporting and formal pleading that the satire seems doubly effective.

Such ridicule of professional jargon and technical pleading can be found in numerous other works of this period. Clients are abused by their attorneys, led from court to court, subjected to endless delays in litigation and growing attorneys' bills, misled in the first place that success is inevitable or, if the client seems ready to compromise, that success is just around the corner. Counsel informs his client that his case will "come on" at the next hearing, or that new evidence of some importance has come to light, or that a number of precedents have been found which seal the case for the client, or that the defendant is merely stalling for time in the very hope that the plaintiff will swallow his indignities. Attorneys and counselors employ legal jargon to impress or confuse, or even intimidate, their clients. Feignall, in Edward Phillips's *The Mock Lawyer*, even impresses an ignorant justice with an outburst of typical legal jargon: "*Noverint universi per praesent. quod idem* Thomas Goosequill, *praedict. Paroch. Sant. Marg. West. Comitatu* Mid. *Scilicet ... Item, Omnia Bona & Catella Messuagia Tenementa Hortos Toftos, & Boschos, Pomaria, Oviariaria, Apiaria, Aviaria, Piscaria, & caet.*" Later when Justice Lovelaw expresses concern about the effect of the recent act abolishing Latin and Law French, Feignall, the mock lawyer, reassures him: "No, no, no, we Lawyers should still have our *Quid pro Quo*, we should still have Leases, Releases, Abeiances, Assignments, Apportionments, Extinguishments, Replevins, Writs, Plaints, Returns, Relations, Declarations, Confirmations, Reservations,—Then, Sir, Actions on the Case, Trover and Conversions, *Nisi Prius's, Certiorari's, Habeas Corpus's,* Pleas, Barrs, Replications, Rejoinders, Surrejoinders, Rebutters, Surrebutters, Demurrers—"[63] The mock lawyer is perfectly correct. The justice's misgivings are clearly unfounded, as subsequent legal history and law satire have shown.

In many of the satirical works discussed, the author places himself above or outside the world inhabited by his legal characters. Oliver Goldsmith's Citizen is a visitor from a saner and wiser society on the other side of the world. Fielding's Vinegar is a self-appointed judge of morality and good manners who sits in judgment on "whatever is wicked, hateful, absurd, or ridiculous."[64] Gulliver is a reporter of European customs to individuals living in ideal and imaginary worlds. The novelist Tobias Smollett often poses as a kind of Don Quixote who determines all cases in terms of ancient chivalric standards and the code of the

British gentleman.[65] Gay usually places his criticisms of the law in the mouths of footpads, highwaymen, and bawds whose own raw sense of honor and justice is pitted against the fraud and depravity of legal authorities. George Stevens masquerades as a prominent scholar who delivers "lectures on heads."[66] In other words, the satirist speaks from a point of detachment and rarely enters the world of absurd law except as observer and commentator. There is good reason for this strategy, for the victim of the ignoramus must be as stupid as the deceiver. In fact, the very success of the ignoramus lawyer depends wholly upon a plentiful supply of ignorant and gullible clients, whose greed and belligerence outweigh common sense. In this world, of course, the ignoramus is a kind of non-lawyer who utters perpetual nonsense. For this character, as Stevens jovially describes it, "The essence of law is altercation, for the law can altercate, fulminate, deprecate, irritate, and go on at any rate:—now the quintessence of the law has, according to its name, five parts. The first is the *beginning,* or *insipiendum*; the second, *uncertainty,* or *dubitendum*; the third, *delay,* or *puzzliendum*; fourthly, *replication,* without *endum*; and fifthly, *monstrum,* and *horrendum.*"[67] In such a world, anything is possible, even a bull going to law against a boat and being nonsuited by a water-bailiff.

Even in the serious fiction of the early eighteenth century, the ignorance of lawyers, uneducated not only in the law but also in the three Rs, remains largely representational. The utter dependence of justices and attorneys upon their clerks is a typical feature of plots involving country justice. Although Fielding's mature novels are not centrally concerned with law criticism, the novelist can scarcely resist an occasional ironic comment about the low ebb of legal learning, as B. M. Jones has indicated.[68] His minor law figures are guilty of all the familiar absurdities and are not much subtler than their forebears, such as Hocus, Puzzle, Brief, and Latitat. They pose no serious threat to anyone's happiness but serve primarily as temporary blocking figures to the protagonists. The bawdy justices are often the rural counterparts of characters like Squeezum, such as Lawyer Scout in *Joseph Andrews,* who is responsible for the hilarious "*depusition of* James Scout, *layer, and* Thomas Trotter, *yeoman, taken befor mee, on his magesty's justasses of the piece for* Zumerzetshire" (4.5). The whole deposition is badly written and misspelled because the unfortunate "justass" had to write it himself without the help of his clerk. Squire Western in *Tom Jones* furnishes an interesting variation upon the theme of the ignorant justice, for, although he is basically warmhearted and humane, he too depends upon his clerk who "had a qualification, which no clerk to a justice ought to be without, namely, some understanding in the laws of this realm." When Mrs. Western, in a moment of rage, wants to have a pert servant committed to Bridewell, the squire consults his clerk who objects to the proposal. The squire accepts the advice, and when his wife cites the contrary example of a London justice who commits servants upon the request of their betters, the impestuous Western remains firm in his sense of justice: "Like enough," cries the squire, "it may be so in London; but the law is different in the country" (7.9). That the law in rural England was not always so humane, however, is demonstrated by the plight of the unfortunate Partridge, or by the successful machinations of Blifil, aided by the pettifogging Dowling, which threaten temporarily the happiness of Tom and Sophia.

Another interesting variation upon the ignoramus lawyer who constantly spouts law terms is Tom Clarke in Smollett's *Sir Launcelot Greaves* (1762). Like the quixotic squire, young Tom Clarke is an idealistic character who has devoted his career as an attorney to aiding helpless widows and orphans. He does most of his work, we are told, in forma pauperis, and he is so aware of the low repute of his profession that he never confesses that he is an attorney without blushing.[69] Tom's legal comments, however, are usually dull and prolix, filled with tautology, technical jargon, and citations of statutes and precedents. In fact, this trait becomes his chief charm for the reader as a kind of winning and amusing tediousness, as for example when he informs Dolly that he will "seize" her in tail and make a settlement upon her, or when he explains to his uncle why he should not have made so free with Sir Launcelot's armor:

> "Taking away another man's moveables, (said he) and personal goods against the will of the owner, is *furtum* and felony according to the statute: different indeed from robbery, which implies putting in fear on the king's highway, *in alta via regis violenter, & felonice captum & asportatum in magnum terrorem, &c.* for if robbery be laid in the indictment as done *in quadam via pedestri,* in a footpath, the offender will not be ousted of his clergy. It must be *in alta via regis;* for the king's high-stream is all the same as the king's highway." (60-61)

It matters little that the squire has no intention of demanding ultimate justice against his old friend the captain. The opportunity has arisen for Tom to display his learning, and everyone is delighted to hear him out. When the real crisis occurs, however, the genial attorney puts the egregious Justice Gobble to ignominious rout when he threatens an action *in Banco Regis* for *falsum imprisonamentum.* The ignorant old justice, thoroughly intimidated by Tom's vocabulary, has no other recourse but to invite the injured parties all to "a bit of bacon." In the words of Stevens, Gobble chickens out at the prospect of the pure *"horrendum"* which might ensue from Tom's expertise in *"puzzliendum"* without *"endum."* He is the victim of an ignoramus type who in all other respects has emancipated himself from the conventions normally associated with law satire.

um, types with roots in the burlesque poetry and the stage satire of the early eighteenth century. In Fielding's mature novels, the two-dimensional portraiture fades, the personified names disappear, and the representational elements are fused into individual characters to produce much more complex personalities like Dowling and Squire Western in *Tom Jones* but particularly the treacherous Murphy in *Amelia,* a diabolical lawyer to be sure, though not to be explained purely in terms of conventional representations of the lawyer since his avarice stems from a fully developed personality.[2]

This is not to say that the lawyer-devil entirely disappears, but he must be tracked more assiduously among the lesser poets of the late eighteenth and nineteenth centuries, such as George Crabbe, William Gifford, Robert Southey, Thomas Moore, and the scores of would-be poets who contributed satirical pieces to magazines or published in the popular press, such as the vituperative Reginald Blewitt's *The Court of Chancery* which may well have colored Dickens's treatment of that court in *Bleak House.*

Romantic and Victorian authors did not pay much attention to the lawyer as ignoramus, for their more serious reforming spirit allowed little scope for the development of comic portraiture. Cunning and mean-spirited pettifoggers like Quirk, Gammon, Dockwrath, and Wakem do, of course, deliberately interlard their conversation with legal terminology as a means of intimidating or impressing their clients, but the same might be said for the good and honorable lawyers, like Furnivall and Graham, who supervise their downfall. In fact, if the ignoramus type had a future in later literature, it is chiefly to be found in such popular and burlesque works as *The Pleader's Guide, The Bar, The Templar, Causidicus: A Poetical Lash, Law: A Brief,* and *A Peep at the Wiltshire Assizes* (some of which were written by lawyers), or occasionally in popular drama and farce such as Boucicault's *London Assurance,* Albery's *Wig and Gown,* and H. J. Bryon's *The Thumbscrew.*

By the mid nineteenth century, of course, a great many massive reforms had already begun to sweep "the Augean stables of the law," as John Stuart Mill phrased it, leading up to the climactic Judicature Acts of 1873-1874. It may very well be that the work of men like Warren, Lytton, Dickens, and Reade added to the swell of public opinion which ushered in these reforms, but whatever our suspicions might suggest about such matters, it will be as well to reserve judgment until the story is told.

Epilogue

IN LATER LITERATURE, it is possible to trace the echoes and vestiges of earlier satirical representations of the common lawyer in the works of Romantic and Victorian authors, such as Edgeworth's attorney Case (*Simple Susan*), Warren's Caleb Quirk and Oily Gammon (*Ten Thousand a Year*), Dickens's Brass (*The Old Curiosity Shop*) or Tulkinghorn (*Bleak House*), Eliot's Wakem (*Mill on the Floss*), and Trollope's Dockwrath (*Orley Farm*), all of whom bear the unmistakable marks of the pettifogger. In the later development of the novel, however, authors characteristically concentrate upon specific legal problems, frequently introducing lawsuits and trials explored in intimate detail, such as *Tittlemouse v. Aubrey* in *Ten Thousand a Year* (1839), *Jarndyce v. Jarndyce*, the great Chancery suit in *Bleak House* (1853), or the forgery trial of Lady Mason in *Orley Farm* (1862). The flat legal characterization of the earlier periods becomes considerably more complex as the traditional representations of the common lawyer are drawn into the critical orbit of the age of reform sparked by men like Bentham, Romilly, and Brougham. In fact, a great many of the greater novelists of the Romantic and Victorian periods believed in the efficacy of the novel in the promotion of a wide range of legal reforms: the use of collusive actions in Lord Lytton's *Night and Morning* and Warren's *Ten Thousand A Year*; penal reforms and the death penalty in Lytton's *Paul Clifford* and *Eugene Aram,* or Dickens's *Barnaby Rudge* and *Oliver Twist*; the injustices of debtor's prisons in Dickens's *Pickwick Papers* or *Little Dorrit*; the questions arising from forfeited mortgages and the law of entails in Emily Brontë's *Wuthering Heights* or George Eliot's *Felix Holt*; or even the law relating to bigamy and mental illness in Charlotte Brontë's *Jane Eyre* or Charles Reade's *Griffith Gaunt* and *Hard Cash*.[1] The lawyer-devil representation virtually disappears as a distinct convention after 1750, when the typical features become submerged and modified in the creation of more realistic and psychologically lifelike legal characters. Such a trend, in fact, is noticeable in the novels of Henry Fielding, whose earlier works had contained numerous representational figures such as Brief, Wilding, Pounce, and Squeez-

Notes

Chapter 1. Satire and the Law: Grounds for Criticism

1. Both W. H. Auden poems are from his *Collected Shorter Poems, 1927-1957* (London: Faber and Faber, 1966), 154-56.

2. Sir Morris Finer, Q. C., "The Legal Profession," in *What's Wrong With the Law?* ed. Michael Zander (Montreal: McGill University Press, 1970), 45.

3. F. W. Maitland, *Collected Papers* (Cambridge: Cambridge University Press, 1911), 1:466.

4. *The Complete Works of St. Thomas More,* ed. Edward Surtz, S. J. and J. H. Hexter (New Haven: Yale University Press, 1965), 4:61-81, 195. For a dramatization of More's legendary career as the upright judge who teaches by example, see *Sir Thomas More* (c. 1595) in *The Shakespeare Apocrypha: Being a Collection of Fourteen Plays Which Have Been Ascribed to Shakespeare,* ed. C. F. Tucker Brooke (Oxford: Clarendon Press, 1908), 383-420.

5. *The Complete Essays of Montaigne,* ed. Donald M. Frame (Stanford: Stanford University Press, 1958), 816.

6. The first statutes enacted against maintenance were Westminster I, c. 25 ("No officer of the King by themselves, nor by any other, shall maintain pleas, suits, or matters hanging in the King's courts, for lands, tenements, or other things, for to have part or profit thereof by covenant made between them; and he that doth shall be punished at the King's pleasure."); Westminster II, c. 36 and c. 49; and 28 Edw. I, c. 11. For fuller discussion of these statutory provisions, see P. H. Winfield, *The History of Conspiracy and Abuse of Legal Procedure* (Cambridge: Cambridge University Press, 1921), passim, and John H. Baker, "Solicitors and the Law of Maintenance," *CLJ* 32 (April 1973): 56-80.

7. *The Queene's Arcadia,* in *The Complete Works of Samuel Daniel,* ed. A. B. Grosart (1885-1896; reprint, New York: Russell and Russell, 1963), 3:247-48 (lines 970-73, 981-90).

8. William Shakespeare, *The Tempest* in *The Oxford Shakespeare: Complete Works,* ed. W. J. Craig (Oxford: Oxford University Press, 1955), 2.1.154-63.

9. Robert Burton, *The Anatomy of Melancholy* (London: Everyman's Library, 1932), 1:101.

10. Fulke Greville, *The Remains Being Poems of Monarchy and Religion,* ed. G. A. Wilkes (Oxford: Oxford University Press, 1955), stanzas 261-62.

11. Cited from John H. Baker, *An Introduction to English Legal History* (London: Butterworth, 1971), 294. For further discussion of the relationships between common lawyers and the Puritans in the pre-Civil War period, see J. D. Eusden, *Puritans, Lawyers, and Politics in Early Seventeenth-Century England,* Yale Studies in Religious Education, vol. 23 (New Haven: Yale University Press, 1958); W. J. Jones, *Politics and the Bench: The Judges and the Origins of the English Civil Wars* (London: Allen and Unwin, 1971); B. P. Levack, *The Civil Lawyers in England, 1603-1641* (Oxford: Oxford University Press, 1973).

12. *Gulliver's Travels,* in *The Prose Works of Jonathan Swift,* ed. Herbert Davis (Oxford: Basil Blackwell, 1965), 11:136.

13. *The Autobiography of Anthony Trollope* (Oxford: Oxford University Press, 1953), 81-82; James Sutherland, *English Satire* (Cambridge: Cambridge University Press, 1958), 15-18.

14. J. Huizinga, *Homo Ludens* (London: Routledge, 1958), 76-78, in the chapter "Play and Law" stresses the agonistic and competitive elements of the law and also suggests that its highly formalized rules are most typical of all archaic systems of law. Although the fundamental roots remain, the rules are moralized and complicated in later periods of legal development when rational argument displaces appeals to the supernatural and when the danger is recognized that winning may become the sole aim of the contestants.

15. G. R. Owst, *Literature and Pulpit in Medieval England* (Oxford: Blackwell, 1966). See also James Sutherland, *English Satire* (Cambridge: Cambridge University Press, 1958); Matthew Hodgart, *Satire* (New York: McGraw-Hill, 1973); Alvin Kernan, *The Cankered Muse* (New Haven: Yale University Press, 1959); and John Peter, *Complaint and Satire in Early English Literature* (Oxford: Oxford University Press, 1956).

16. The following discussion is indebted to Jill Mann's *Chaucer and Medieval Estates Satire* (Cambridge: Cambridge University Press, 1973) and John A. Yunck, *The Lineage of Lady Meed* (Notre Dame: Notre Dame Press, 1963).

17. For the many judicial roles performed by churchmen, the knighthood, and the landed gentry, see J. P. Dawson, *The History of Lay Judges* (Cambridge: Harvard University Press, 1960).

18. Rudolf Kirk, "References to the Law in *Piers the Plowman,*" *PMLA* 48 (June 1933):322-27.

19. Owst, *Literature and Pulpit,* 338-49.

20. *The Voice of One Crying,* in *The Major Latin Works of John Gower,* ed. E. W. Stockton (Seattle: Washington University Press, 1962), 220-22.

21. Alan Harding writes that "in Henry I's reign there were already complaints of 'the avarice and sinister and odious activity of the legal experts' whose 'new way of pleading' obscured 'the certain truth of the law' and involved legal process 'in so many and great anxieties and deceits, that men avoid these actions and the uncertain dice of pleas'" (*The Law Courts of Medieval England* [London: Allen and Unwin, 1973], 84). See also F. W. Maitland's introduction to *The Mirror of Justices,* ed. W. J. Whitaker, S. S. vol. 7 (London: Selden Society, 1893), xlvii-ix; *Leges Henrici Primi,* ed. L. J. Downer (Oxford: Oxford University Press, 1972), 99; and *The Chronicle of Bury St. Edmunds, 1212-1301,* ed. Antonia Gransden (Oxford: Oxford University Press, 1964), 47.

22. Samuel E. Thorne traces the beginning of Tudor commercial expansion and related changes in the land law to the late Middle Ages in "Tudor Social Transformation and Legal Change," *New York University Law Review* 26 (January 1951):10-23. For Parkhurst's couplet, see my Harvard dissertation, "Ferdinando Parkhurst's *Ignoramus, the Academical-Lawyer: A Critical Edition*" (Cambridge, 1970): IA:3 (Prologue, lines 11-12).

23. *The English Works of Wycliff,* ed. F. D. Matthew, EETS, o.s. vol. 74 (London, 1880), 182. Wycliff's main interest in the common law was as a ready means of support for his own program of ecclesiastical reform. For a useful discussion of this and other issues, see William Farr, *John Wyclif as Legal Reformer,* Studies in the History of Christian Thought, vol. 10 (Leiden: E. J. Brill, 1974).

24. V. J. Scattergood, *Politics and Poetry in the Fifteenth Century* (New York: Barnes and Noble, 1971), 306.

25. *Peter Idley's Instructions to His Son,* ed. Charlotte D'Evelyn (Boston: Heath, 1935), 83, 151, and passim.

26. E. W. Ives, "The Reputation of the Common Lawyers in English Society, 1450-1550," *University of Birmingham Historical Journal* 7 (June 1960):130-161; *The Book of Vices and Virtues,* ed. W. Nelson Francis, EETS, o.s. vol. 217 (London, 1942), 34-36.

27. Ives, "Reputation of Common Lawyers," 145-61; *Peter Idley's Instructions,* 151-52; and More, *Utopia,* 4:61-81; *Henry Brinklow's Complaynt of Roderyck Mors,* ed. J. M. Cowper, EETS, e.s. vol. 22 (London, 1874), 18; Philip Stubbes, *Anatomy of Abuses,* ed. F. J. Furnivall, New Shakespeare Society Publications, ser. 6, no. 6 (London, 1879), 1:79; Thomas Starkey, *A Dialogue between Reginald Pole and Thomas Lupset,* ed. K. Burton (London: Chatto, 1948), 122-23.

28. The Year Books mention several cases involving attorneys who accepted money from maintainers to bribe jurors and witnesses (e.g. in 11 Hen. VI, f. 10; 36 Hen. Vi, ff. 27-29; and 6 Edw. IV, f. 5). However, cases of this kind did not attract much attention from the Year Book reporters unless they involved some new point of procedural difficulty. A complete review of the plea rolls is needed. For further details and a review of *Somerton's Case* (1433), see C. H. S. Fifoot, *History and Sources of the Common Law: Tort and Contract* (London: Stevens, 1949), 90-91, 343-44, Fifoot lists two writs against ambidextry from Rastell's *Entries* (1574), the first *"vers Counsellor,"* the second *"vers Attorney ou Counsellor"* who *"falso et fraudulenter decepit ad damnum"* the plaintiff of so much money. Presumably, these *accions sur le case* are of later development and thus more specific in their allegations than the older actions on the case *pro deceptione.* Alan Harding tells the story of Gilbert Sherman, an "attorney at the Common Law and therefore able to engage in law-suits without charge to himself" who "was accused in Star Chamber of beginning suits against his neighbours and then accepting payment to leave them in peace" (*A Social History of English Law* [London: Allen and Unwin, 1966], 211). Contemporary literature, according to Harding, is filled with accounts of attorneys and solicitors who were disciplined for breaches of professional ethics. The customary punishment included fines, the loss of ears, the slitting of noses, the pillory, and the humiliating ceremony of being struck from the court rolls and being pitched headlong over the bar.

29. *The Supposes,* in *The Complete Works of George Gascoigne* (London: Putnam, 1907), 1: 193, 211, 238. Gascoigne's translation of Ariosto's comedy was first performed at Gray's Inn in 1566.

30. Edward F. J. Tucker provides fuller discussion of the importance of Ruggle's satirical comedy in "*Ignoramus* and Seventeenth-Century Satire of the Law," *Harvard Library Bulletin* 19 (July 1971): 314-30.

31. *Ignoramus, Comoedia: Scriptore Georgio Ruggle, A.M.,* ed. John Sidney Hawkins (London, 1787), 44-46, cited hereafter as Hawkins.

32. Ives, "Reputation of Common Lawyers," 130-33. For a fuller account of Tudor-Stuart criticism of the common law language, see E. F. J. Tucker, "*Ignoramus* and Humanistic Criticism of the Language of the Common Law," *Renaissance Quarterly* 30 (Autumn 1977):341-50.

33. Quoted from Treby's edition of *Dyer's Reports* (1688) by Alan Harding, *Social History of English Law,* 205.

34. Sir Thomas Smith, *De Repulica Anglorum* (1583), ed. L. Alston (Cambridge: Cambridge University Press, 1906), 49-50; *The Learned Reading of Sir Francis Bacon* (London, 1642), sigs. C3v-C4r.

35. Edward F. J. Tucker, "The Harvard Manuscript of Parkhurst's *Ignoramus,*" *Harvard Library Bulletin* 19 (January 1971):5-7.

36. M. B. Forbes, *Clare College, 1326-1926* (Cambridge: Cambridge University Press, 1928-1930), 2:534.

37. Elizabeth M. Thomson, *The Chamberlain Letters* (New York: Putnam, 1965), 132-33. The letter is dated 20 May 1615.

38. Ibid.

Chapter 2. Satire, Legal Education, and the Inns

1. Hermann Cohen, *A History of the English Bar and Attornatus to 1450* (London: Carswell, 1929), 112-60.

2. T. F. T. Plucknett's *Early English Legal Literature* (Cambridge: Cambridge University Press, 1958) furnishes the best brief review of this literature.

3. Samuel E. Thorne traces the earliest readings to 1427 (by Gilbert Haltoft) and 1431 (by Master Moyle) but conjectures that such exercises may have been introduced near the beginning of the century, in his introduction to *Readings and Moots at the Inns of Court in the Fifteenth Century,* SS vol. 71 [London: Selden Society, 1952]).

4. For Chaucer's supposed connections with the Inner Temple, see D. S. Bland, "Chaucer and the Inns of Court: A Reexamination," *English Studies* 33 (1952):145-55; and Edith Rickert, "Was Chaucer a Student at the Inner Temple?" *Manly Anniversary Studies in Language and Literature* (Chicago: Chicago University Press, 1923), 20-31. All references to Chaucer's works are from *The Works of Geoffrey Chaucer,* ed. F. N. Robinson (Boston: Houghton Mifflin, 1957).

5. J. M. Manly, *Some New Light on Chaucer* (New York: Holt, 1926), 131.

6. Lothario dei Segni, *On the Misery of the Human Condition,* ed. Donald R. Howard (Indianapolis: Bobbs-Merrill, 1969), 36-37.

7. Richard de Bury, *Philolbiblon,* ed. E. C. Thomas (Oxford: Blackwell, 1960), 117-21; *English Works of Wycliff,* 157.

8. Sir John Fortescue, *A Learned Commendation of the Politique Lawes of England,* trans. Robert Mulcaster (London, 1599), sig. D5r. This work was written at some time between 1465 and 1471 for the instruction of Prince Edward, son of Henry VI.

9. *The Diary of John Manningham,* ed. Robert P. Sorlien (Hanover, N.H.: University Press of New England, 1976), 55, 58, 59, 61, 67, 71, 73, passim; Edmund Heward, *Matthew Hale* (London: Hale, 1972), 67.

10. A. W. B. Simpson, "The Early Constitution of Gray's Inn," *CLJ* 34 (April 1975):131-50; W. R. Prest, *The Inns of Court Under Elizabeth I and the Early Stuarts, 1590-1640* (Totowa, N.J.: Rowman and Littlefield, 1972), 1-21.

11. H. H. Bellot, "The Jurisdiction of the Inns of Court over the Inns of Chancery," *LQR* 26 (August 1910):384-99. Few Chancery readings have survived, and even fewer found their way into print.

12. The idea of the third university was popularized by Sir George Buck's "The Third Universitie of England" published as an appendix to John Stow, *The Annales of England,* ed. E. Howes (London, 1615), 958-69. Stow himself had died in 1605. E. W. Ives, "The Law and Lawyers," *Shakespeare Survey 17,* ed. Allardyce Nicoll (Cambridge: Cambridge University Press, 1964), 78.

13. F. J. Finkelpearl, *John Marston of the Middle Temple* (Cambridge: Harvard University Press, 1969), 25; Ives, "Law and Lawyers," 78-80; Prest, *Inns of Court,* 153-58.

14. A. W. Green, *The Inns of Court and Early English Drama* (New Haven: Yale University Press, 1931), 17-21.

15. Marie Axton, *The Queene's Two Bodies: Drama and the Elizabethan Succession* (London: Royal Historical Society, 1977), 39-47, passim, discusses the continuing importance of *Gorboduc* as a commentary upon the delicate question of royal succession during the reign of Elizabeth.

16. Green, *The Inns of Court,* 6-8; Alfred Harbage, *Shakespeare's Audience* (New York: Columbia University Press, 1941), 80-81. Geoffrey Bullough, "Donne the Man of Law," in *Just So Much Honor,* ed. P. A. Fiore (University Park, Pa.: Pennsylvania State University Press, 1972), 66-68; Baird W. Whitlock, *John Hoskyns, Serjeant-at-Law* (Washington: University Press of America, 1982), 381-419.

17. Finkelpearl, *John Marston,* 42-43. See chapter 5 below for further discussion of these satires and the use of legal jargon in love poetry.

18. Verses quoted from Prest, *Inns of Court,* 156.

19. *The Plain Dealer,* in *The Complete Plays of William Wycherley,* ed. Gerald Weales (New York: Norton, 1972), 4.1.254-55, 3.1.542-44.

20. *The Phoenix,* in *The Works of Thomas Middleton,* ed. A. H. Bullen (1885-1886; reprint, New York: Ames Press, 1964), 1.6.111-12. Unless otherwise noted, all subsequent citations from Middleton are to this edition. For references to Jonson's works, see *Ben Jonson: Complete Critical Edition,* ed. C. E. Herford and Percy and Evelyn Simpson (Oxford: Oxford University Press, 1925-1951). The quotation is from *The Poetaster,* 1.2.123-24. Volumes 3 and 4 of the Oxford *Jonson* are now supplemented by G. A. Wilkes's edition of *The Complete Plays of Ben Jonson* (Oxford University Press, 1981-82), which provides a modernized version of the Herford-Simpson texts. Ruggle's strongest censure of ignoramus lawyers is found in Musaeus's speech to Trico: "*Scientiae, / Nisi Ignoramus, hostis nemo est. Ignoramus igitur illiusque similes, / Qui ecclesiam & academias pessumdatas cupiunt*" (Nobody is so great an enemy to learning as Ignoramus. It is Ignoramus, therefore, and such as he who wish to put down the church and the colleges) (Hawkins, 105).

21. *The Devil's Law-Case,* in *The Complete Works of John Webster,* ed. F. L. Lucas

(New York: Oxford University Press, 1937), 4.1.36-39. Lucas dates the play between 1619 and 1621 (2:246).

22. For references to Parkhurst's translation of Ruggle's play, see my Harvard dissertation, "Ferdinando Parkhurst's *Ignoramus, The Academical-Lawyer: A Critical Edition*" (Cambridge, Mass., 1970).

23. Prest, *Inns of Court,* 138-43.

24. George Whetstone, *A Mirour for Magestrates of Cyties* (London, 1584), sig. H4r; Sir Thomas Overbury, "A Fantastique Innes of Court Man," in *The Overburian Characters,* ed. W. J. Paylor (Oxford: Blackwell, 1936), 45-46. A fantastique was the earlier version of the Restoration fop.

25. Francis Lenton, *Characterismi: or, Lentons Leasures* (London, 1631), sigs. F4v-F5v.

26. Jasper Mayne, *The Citie Match* (Oxford, 1639). All turns out well for the Inns-a-Court blades, for Plotwell's heavy expenditures and his "Temple Scores," as his uncle Warehouse discovers, have gone mostly toward the preservation of his sister's estate.

27. David Barrey, *Ram-Alley, or Merrie Trickes* (London, 1611), sig. D4v.

28. Thomas Middleton, *The Works of Thomas Middleton,* ed. Alexander Dyce (London, 1840), 5:547-603; Prest, *Inns of Court,* 91-100; David Matthews, *The Social Structure of Caroline England* (Oxford: Oxford University Press, 1948), 57.

29. Simpson, "Early Constitution of Gray's Inn," 141.

30. See "The Publisher's Preface Directed to the Young Students of the Common Law," in Henry Rolle, *Un Abridgement des Plusiers Cases et Resolutions del Common Ley* (London, 1668), 1:sigs.ar-cv

31. *Lawyerus Bootatus & Spurratus: or, The Long Vacation* (London, 1691), sig. A2v. The lawyerus is, of course, defying orders *not* to wear boots and spurs in hall.

32. Sir Frederick Pollock, "Fiction Theory," in *Jurisprudence and Legal Essays,* ed. A. L. Goodhart (London: St. Martin's Press, 1961), 220; According to Sir William Holdsworth, "At the beginning of the eighteenth century the Inns had ceased to be educational institutions. Educationally they had become . . . 'a university in a state of decay'" (*HEL* 12:16). Roscoe Pound, *The Lawyer from Antiquity to Modern Times* (St. Paul, Minn.: West Publishing, 1953), 91; Harding, *Social History of English Law,* 289.

33. G. W. Keeton, *Shakespeare's Legal and Political Background* (London: Isaac Pitman, 1967), 12-13; H. H. Bellot, "The Exclusion of the Attorneys from the Inns of Court," *LQR* 26 (April 1910):137-45; J. H. Baker, "Counsellors and Barristers," *CLJ* 27 (November 1969):222-29.

34. Michael Birks, *Gentleman of the Law* (London: Carswell, 1960), 106-10.

35. Robert Robson, *The Attorney in Eighteenth-Century England* (Cambridge: Cambridge University Press, 1959), 52.

36. Robson, *The Attorney,* 12-13.

37. *The Diary of Dudley Ryder, 1715-16,* ed. William Matthews (London: Methuen, 1939), 71-72, 85, 106-7, 138.

38. W. Scawen Blunt writes "All those named in the Diary seem to have contented themselves with heavy drinking, much card playing and occasional entertainments at the Horsham public rooms," in "Extracts from Mr. John Baker's Horsham Diary," *Sussex Archaeological Collections* 52 (1944):41.

39. *Diary of Dudley Ryder,* 106-7.

40. Joseph Addison and Richard Steele, *The Spectator,* ed. Donald F. Bond (Oxford: Oxford University Press, 1965), 1:209, 2:272, 3:402-3.

41. For parallels between Fielding's works and legal career, see B. M. Jones, *Henry Fielding, Novelist and Magistrate* (London: Allen, 1933).

42. *Temple Beau,* in *The Complete Works of Henry Fielding,* ed. W. E. Henley (New York: Harper, 1902), 5.6. Since the plays are characterized by numerous brief scenes, and since Henley provides no line numbers, I supply only act and scene references within the text. Citations from the novels are taken from specific editions as noted below.

43. Fielding, *The Temple Beau,* 15:18-19.

44. Blackstone was called to the bar at the Middle Temple only eight years after the publication of *The Champion.* For his career at law, see D. A. Lockmiller, *Sir William Blackstone* (Chapel Hill: University of North Carolina Press, 1938); Paul Lucas, "Blackstone and the Reform of the Legal Profession," *EHR* 77 (July 1962):456-89.

45. To commemorate his momentous decision to concentrate upon legal studies, Blackstone wrote a poem entitled "The Lawyer Bids Farewell to His Muse," included as appendix 1 in Lockmiller, *Sir William Blackstone,* 191-94. Robert Lloyd, *Poems* (London, 1762), 129-37.

Chapter 3. Representations of Pettifoggery

1. *The Oxford English Dictionary,* s.v. "pettifogger," lists William Bulleyn's *Dialogue against the Fever Pestilence* (1564) as the earliest work using this term.

2. *Leycesters Commonwealth* (London, 1641), 178, equates the promoter and the pettifogger as types who enrich themselves by other men's ruin. This anonymous tract is believed to have been written in 1584.

3. *James the Fourth,* in *The Life and Complete Works of Robert Greene,* ed. A. B. Grosart (London: Published privately, 1881-1883), 13:304-8 (5.4).

4. *The Book of Vices and Virtues,* 39-40.

5. *Middle English Sermons,* ed. W. O. Ross, EETS, o.s. vol. 209 (Oxford, 1940), 101.

6. *The Book of Vices and Virtues,* 35.36.

7. Cohen believes that "the venal practitioner whom the literary men denounce was comparatively a novelty" (*History of the English Bar,* 161). Bearing in mind the strategy of satirical exaggeration, one has to agree that there were possibly fewer dishonest lawyers than the literary picture suggests.

8. Harding, *Law Courts of Medieval England,* 114.

9. Scattergood, *Politics and Poetry,* 316-25.

10. H. S. Bennett, *The Pastons and Their England* (Cambridge: Cambridge University Press, 1922), 165-92. Holdsworth writes, "The forms of law and physical violence had come to be merely alternative instruments to be used as seemed most expedient. This was the reason why a knowledge of the law was at this time so widely diffused. It was as necessary for self-protection as a knowledge of warlike weapons. The law was no longer a shield for the weak and oppressed—rather it was a sword for the unscrupulous" (*HEL* 2:348).

11. *Secunda Pastorum,* in *The Wakefield Pageants in the Towneley Cycle,* ed. A. C. Cawley, Old and Middle English Texts (Manchester: Manchester University Press, 1958), 43-44, lines 10-45; and *Wisdom Who Is Christ,* in *The Macro Plays,* ed. F. J. Furnivall and Alfred W. Pollard, EETS, e.s. vol. 91 (London, 1904), lines 674-83. Also see Thomas Hoccleve, *The Regement of Princes,* ed. F. J. Furnivall, EETS, o.s. vol. 73 (London, 1925),

lines 2780-2835, for a lengthy account of contemporary lawlessness. Arnold Williams, *The Characterization of Pilate in the Towneley Plays* (East Lansing: Michigan State University Press, 1950), 37-51, uses contemporary materials to illustrate the corruption of the law by unscrupulous lawyers and judges. In *Gamelyn*, of course, the corrupt judge is eventually apprehended, tried, and hanged.

12. J. G. Bellamy, *Crime and Public Order in the Later Middle Ages* (London: Routledge and Kegan Paul, 1973), 22, 99, 199. Bellamy's chapter on the activities of criminal bands (69-88) furnishes essential insights into the nature of medieval lawlessness.

13. Thomas G. Barnes, "Star Chamber Mythology," *AJLH* 5 (January 1961):1-11; and "Due Process and Slow Process," *AJLH* 6 (1962):221-49, 315-46.

14. Harding, *Social History of English Law*, 244-46.

15. Sir John Davies of Hereford, "Epigram 168," *The Scourge of Folly*, in *The Complete Works*, ed. A. B. Grosart (1876; reprint, New York: AMS Press, 1967), 2:27.

16. Thomas G. Barnes, "Star Chamber Litigants and Their Counsel, 1596-1641," in *Legal Records and the Historian*, ed. J. H. Baker (London: Royal Historical Society, 1978), 1-28. A statistical survey of the classes of litigants bringing suits in Star Chamber is provided in table 1, p. 10.

17. Birks, *Gentlemen of the Law*, 87-88; see also W. J. Jones. *The Elizabethan Court of Chancery* (Oxford: Clarendon Press, 1967), 314-17, for a useful commentary on the unscrupulous conduct of litigants in Chancery and the common law courts.

18. William Bulleyn observes that "fellows are so brain sick now-a-days if they have but x shillings, yea, though they do borrow it, will be two or three times a year at Westmynster Hall" (*A Dialogue against the Fever Pestilence* [London, 1564], sig. H8r); Robert Copland equates litigious conduct with madness (*Highway to the Spital House* [1535-1536], ed. A. V. Judges, in *Elizabethan Underworld* [London: Routledge, 1940], 14), as does Nicholas Breton (*A Mad World My Masters* [London, 1602], sig. Clv).

19. Sir Matthew Hale, *Considerations Touching Amendment or Alterations of Law*, in *A Collection of Tracts Relating to the Law of England*, ed. Francis Hargrave (London, 1787), 1:257.

20. *The Chamberlain Letters*, 138. Chamberlain's own unfortunate experience in Chancery has obviously influenced his opinion in this instance.

21. *A True Relation of a Most Desperate Murder, Committed upon the Body of Sir Iohn Tindall, Knight, One of the Maisters of Chancery*, (London, 1617), sig. A4v.

22. John Clapham, *Elizabeth of England*, ed. Conyers Read and Evelyn Plummer Read (Philadelphia: University of Pennsylvania Press, 1951), 66.

23. *Complete Works of George Gascoigne* 1:47.

24. Richard Bernard, *The Isle of Man: or, The Legall Proceeding in Man-shire against Sinne* (London, 1630), sig. 13r-v.

25. Jones, *The Elizabethan Chancery*, 315.

26. William Harrison, *The Description of England*, ed. George Edelen (Ithaca, N.Y.: Cornell University Press, 1968), 174-75.

27. *Anatomy of Abuses* 1:10-11.

28. Barnabe Rych, *The Honestie of This Age* (London, 1614), sig. B4r-v.

29. Ives, "Reputation of Common Lawyers," 142; Prest, *Inns of Court*, 42-43, 151-52.

30. Thomas Wilson, *The State of England, Anno Dom. 1600*, ed. F.J. Fisher, in *Camden Miscellany XVII*, 3d ser., vol. 52 (London: Camden Society, 1936), 24-25.

31. Brian P. Levack, *The Civil Lawyers in England, 1603-41: A Political Study* (Oxford: Oxford University Press, 1973), 50-66.

32. Davies of Hereford, *Microcosmos,* in *Complete Works* 1:80.

33. Roger Tisdale, *The Lawyer's Philosophy: or, Law Brought to Light* (London, 1622), sigs. C6v-C7v.

34. Burton, *Anatomy of Melancholy* 1:78,83.

35. Ibid., 1:84.

36. Thomas Dekker, *The Seven Deadly Sinnes of London,* ed. H. F. B. Brett-Smith (Oxford: Blackwell, 1922), 15-20.

37. *The Returne of the Knight of the Post from Hell, With the Divels Answere to the Supplication of Pierce Penilesse* (London, 1606), sig. Elr.

38. *Overburian Characters,* 30-32.

39. Ibid., 64-65. See also Webster, *Works* 4:35.

40. John Earle, "An Atturny," in *Micro-cosmographie or A Piece of the World Discovered,* ed. Gwendolen Murphy (Waltham St. Lawrence, England: Golden Cockerel Press, 1928), 54.

41. John Stephens, *Satyrical Essayes* (London, 1615), 280-83.

42. Samuel Butler, "A Pettifogger," in *Characters,* ed. C. W. Daves (Cleveland: Press of Case Western Reserve University, 1970), 240-41: see also Butler's character "A Litigious Man" for interesting parallels to that of the pettifogger (Ibid., 186-87).

43. H. C., "An Honest Lawyer," in *A Cabinet of Characters,* ed. Gwendolen Murphy (London: Oxford University Press, 1925), 333-34. See also Stephens, *Satyrical Essayes,* 155-60, for a similarly idealistic rendering of the honest practitioner.

44. *A Looking-Glasse for All Proud, Ambitious, Covetous, and Corrupt Lawyers* (London, 1646), 1-6.

45. Barbara Shapiro, "Law Reform in Seventeenth Century England," *AJLH* 19 (October 1975):288-97. Mercurius Rhadamanthus, *The Chiefe Iudge of Hell* (London, 1653), with four numbers extant collected among the Thomason Tracts in the British Library.

46. Donald Veall, *The Popular Movement for Law Reform, 1640-1660* (Oxford: Oxford University Press, 1970), 194-97; Stephen F. Black, "*Coram Protectore*: The Judges of Westminster Hall Under the Protectorate of Oliver Cromwell," *AJLH* 20 (January 1976):32-64.

47. *Mercurius Democritus,* no. 53, 27 April 1653, 421. These papers are collected among the Thomason Tracts in The British Library.

48. *To the Supreme Authority the Parliament of the Commonwealth of England: The Humble Petition of Divers Well-Affected People Inhabiting the City of London and Places Adjacent* (London, 1651), 15. This piece is among the Thomason Tracts in the British Library.

49. Hale, *Considerations Touching Amendment* 1:257.

50. Shapiro, "Law Reform in Seventeenth Century England," 305; Sir Matthew Hale, *The History of the Common Law,* ed. Charles M. Gray (Chicago: Chicago University Press, 1971), 111-13.

51. James Puckle, *The Club: or, A Grey-Cap for a Green Head* (Dublin, 1737), 32-34. The first edition of this work appeared much earlier, perhaps in 1700. Irving Browne furnishes a translation of Boileau's "Epistle to the Abbot des Roches" (*Law and Lawyers*

in Literature [Boston: Soule and Bugbee, 1833], 217). See also Matthew Prior, "The Lame and the Blind Disputing the Right to an Oyster Found: The Lawyer Decides the Controversy," in *The Literary Works,* ed. H. Bunker Wright and Monroe K. Spears (Oxford: Oxford University Press, 1959), 1:543. See also *Citizen of the World,* in *Collected Works of Oliver Goldsmith,* ed. Arthur Friedman (Oxford: Oxford University Press, 1966), 2:392-93.

52. Ned Ward, *The London Spy,* ed. Kenneth Fenwick (London: The Folio Society, 1955), 150-51.

53. Ibid., 152. Here the parasitic relationship of the pettifogger to the law is drawn in the final lines of Ward's portrait: "In short, he's a caterpillar upon earth, who grows fat upon the fruits of others' labour; a mere horse-leech in the Law, that when once he is well fasten'd, he will suck a poor client into a deep consumption."

54. Ned Ward, *A Journey to Hell: or, A Visit Paid to the Devil* (London, 1700), sig. Flr-v.

55. Thomas D'Urfey, *The Progress of Honesty: or, A View of Court and City* (London, 1681), sig. B3v.

56. Swift, *Gulliver's Travels* 11:250.

57. Fielding, *Works* 11:205-7.

58. Henry Fielding, *Joseph Andrews and Shamela,* ed. Martin Battestin (Boston: Houghton Mifflin, 1961), 244.

59. Henry Fielding, *The History of Tom Jones, A Foundling* (New York: Random House, 1964), 295.

60. *Historical Poems of the XIVth and XVth Centuries;* ed. R. H. Robbins (New York: Columbia University Press, 1959), 136.

61. W. J. Jones provides an excellent survey of in forma pauperis procedures, some substantiation of their frequent use, and evidence of abuses within the system (*The Elizabethan Chancery,* 323-28).

62. *Historical Poems,* 130-34.

63. John Fletcher, *The Little French Lawyer,* in *The Works of Francis Beaumont and John Fletcher,* ed. A. H. Bullen et. al. (London: G. Bell, 1912), 2.1.

64. *Michaelmas Term,* 1.1.28-30. Tangle in Middleton's *The Phoenix* is another quasi-legal figure who is continually pressed for time, and Wrangle in Drake's *The Sham Lawyer,* pressed by his neighbors for personal favors, exclaims, "Have ye any Business with me? if so, be brief, for I'm full of Business, and every minute's precious" sig. C1v.

65. Earle, *Micro-cosomographie,* 54; K. W., "A Lawyer in Common," in *Confused Characters of Conceited Coxcombs,* ed. J. O. Halliwell-Phillipps (London, 1860), 43-44; Butler, *Characters,* 112.

66. Ward, *London Spy,* 152.

67. Fielding, *Tom Jones,* 297.

Chapter 4. Lawyers in the Case of God v. The Devil

1. *Thraliana: The Diary of Mrs. Hester Lynch Thrale, 1776-1809,* ed. Katherine C. Balderston (London: Oxford University Press, 1942), 200.

2. Gower, *Major Latin Works,* 220-22.

3. *Ignoramus*, 104-5.

4. For Jonson's praise of great lawyers, see his epigrams 14, 31, 32, 33, 46, and 51 in *Ben Jonson* 6:158-61, 185-87, 217, 225.

5. For a fuller discussion of Jonson's knowledge of the law, see Bertil Johansson, *Law and Lawyers in Elizabethan England, As Evidenced in the Plays of Ben Jonson and Thomas Middleton*, Stockholm Studies in English, vol. 18 (Stockholm: Almquist and Wiksell, 1967).

6. *Ignoramus*, 105.

7. Ives, "Reputation of the Common Lawyer," 145; Cohen, *History of the English Bar*, 161, 459.

8. Browne, *Law and Lawyers*, iii-iv.

9. Ward, *Journey to Hell*, sig. A2v.

10. Glenn W. Hatfield, "Quacks, Pettyfoggers, and Parsons: Fielding's Case against the Learned Professions," *Texas Studies in Language and Literature* 9 (January 1967), 69-83.

11. Sir Thomas Elyot, *The Book Named the Governour*, ed. S. E. Lehmberg (London: Everyman Library, 1962), 114-15.

12. S. S., *The Honest Lawyer* (London, 1626), sig. C2r.

13. See characters 12 and 13, 18 and 19 in Alexander Gardyne, *Characters and Essayes* (Aberdeen, 1625), sigs. B3r-B4r, B6v-B7r; Breton's *The Goode and the Badde* (1616), in *A Mirror of Charactery*, ed. Harold Osborne (London: University Tutorial Press, 1933); and the diptych of "An Honest Lawyer" and "A Meere Atturney," in Stephens, *Satyrical Essayes*, 155-60 and 280-83.

14. See "A Reverend Judge," in *Overburian Characters*, 69; Thomas Fuller's "The Good Advocate," in Browne, *Law and Lawyers*, 149-50; Joseph Hall's "Of the Good Magistrate," in *Heaven upon Earth*, ed. Rudolf Kirk (New Brunswick: Rutgers University Press, 1948); and H. C., "The Character of an Honest Lawyer," in *A Cabinet of Characters*, 332-34.

15. H. C., "An Honest Lawyer," 334.

16. Donald Lupton, *London and the Countrey Carbonadoed and Quartered into Several Characters* (London, 1622), 31-35.

17. Lenton, *Characterismi*, sigs. F4v-F5v; Francis Lenton's *The Innes of Court Anagrammatist* (London, 1634) begins with a long passage of praise for the Inns and celebrates the combined efforts of the Inns for their production of Shirley's *The Triumph of Peace* (1634). See the induction to *Michaelmas Term*, in *The Works of Thomas Middleton*, ed. Dyce, 1:411-13. Wye Saltonstall, "The Tearme," in *Picturae Loquentes* (Oxford: Blackwell, 1946), 71-72.

18. Thomas Dekker, *The Seven Deadly Sinnes of London*, ed. H. F. B. Brett-Smith (Oxford: Blackwell, 1922), 15, 28, 49, passim. The sins enter by the seven gates of London, with the lawyers playing a prominent role in the train of followers accompanying many of their "deadly" leaders, such as the "scrambling ignorant *Petti-foggers*" who join with Lying and the cheats who accompany Shaving.

19. *The Book of Vices and Virtues*, 209-10.

20. An anonymous poem in the Cambridge University Library develops this analogy and mentions both the King's Bench and the Court of Common Pleas (MS. Ii.3.8., fol. 147r).

21. Ross, *Middle English Sermons*, 269-71.

22. For an excellent discussion of the criminal mind, the distinction between *actus reus* and *mens rea,* and the early development of the concept of *"malice prepense,"* see J. M. Kaye, "The Early History of Murder and Manslaughter," *LQR* 83 (July 1967):365-95; (October 1967):569-601.

23. W. Nicholas Knight, "The Narrative Unity of Book V of *The Faerie Queene:* 'That Part of Justice Which is Equity,'" *Review of English Studies* 73 (August 1970):267-94.

24. Thomas Gataker, *God's Parley with Princes, With an Appeale from Them to Him* (London, 1620), 54-55. See also the two sermons in John Prideaux, *Christ's Counsell for Ending Law-Cases* (Oxford, 1615). Perhaps the best example of judicial proceedings conducted in heaven, which with complete felicity follows the prescribed Elizabethan procedure for arrest, examination, and prosecution, is furnished in Richard Bernard's *The Isle of Man: of, The Legall Proceeding in Man-shire against Sinne* (London, 1630), "wherein, by way of a continued Allegorie, the chiefe Malefactors disturbing both Church and Common-wealth, are detected and attached; with their Arraignment and Iudiciall triall according to the Lawes of England" (title page). See also Henry Smith's sermons entitled *The Lawyer's Question* and *The Magistrate's Scripture* for a similar use of legal terms in sermons, in *The Works of Henry Smith* (Edinburgh, 1866-1867), 1:355-70, 2:101-32.

25. Bullough, "Donne the Man of Law," 76, 79-83; John Donne's *Devotions upon Emergent Occasions,* ed. John Sparrow (Cambridge: Cambridge University Press, 1923), 15ln. See also *A Sermon Preached at Lincoln's Inn by John Donne,* ed. G. R. Potter (Stanford: Stanford University Press, 1946), 20-25.

26. Quoted from John M. Wallace, *Destiny His Choice: The Loyalism of Andrew Marvell* (Cambridge: Cambridge University Press, 1968), 81. Fuller here refers to Charles I.

27. "The Pilgrimage," in *The Poems of Sir Walter Raleigh,* ed. A. M. C. Latham (London: Routledge, 1951), 50-51. The *angel* was the standard fee charged by most lawyers for initial engagement of their services (6/8d).

28. W. J. Jones explains that "conscience" was technically a vague term. Judicially it embraced the litigant's state of mind, but it was difficult to apply in the absence of clearly defined judicial principles (*The Elizabethan Court of Chancery,* 420-24).

29. Tisdale, *The Lawyer's Philosophy,* sigs. B2r-v.

30. Ibid., sigs. C6v-C7v.

31. G. W. Keeton, *Shakespeare's Legal and Political Background* (London: Isaac Pitman, 1967), 5. W. J. Jones, *Politics and the Bench,* 123-48.

32. Brian Morris, "Satire from Donne to Marvell," in *Metaphysical Poetry,* ed. Malcolm Bradbury and David Palmer (Bloomington: Indiana University Press, 1970), 217-18.

33. See Davies, *Works* 2:242; and *Frondes Caducae* (Edinburgh, 1816), 81.

34. For another view of Davies, see Sorlien's edition of *The Diary of John Manningham,* p. 7-8, passim.

35. John Denham, *The Poetical Works of Sir John Denham,* ed. Theodore H. Banks (New York: Shoestring Press, 1969), 155-58. Denham's father had joined Croke as judges for the dissenting party.

36. Epigram 46 in *Ben Jonson* 7:217, on Sir Edward Coke; see Jonson's epigrams 31 and 32 for praise of Lord Ellesemere, ibid., 7:185-86. Epigram 51 celebrates Bacon's birthday and his recent appointment to the post of Lord Keeper of the Great Seal, ibid.; 7:255; and

for the poet's admiration of Selden, see epigram 14, ibid., 7:158-61. Selden's *The History of Tithes* (1618) was written at the time of Coke's dismissal from the bench, and friends of Ruggle thought that Selden's work was inspired by the success of *Ignoramus* and thus directed at the clergy as a measure of revenge (see Forbes, *Clare College* 2:534).

37. J. H. Baker, "Common Lawyers and the Chancery, 1616," *The Irish Jurist* 4 (Winter 1969):368-92; Jones, *Elizabethan Court of Chancery,* 449-98; and J. W. Gough, *Fundamental Law in English Constitutional History* (Oxford: Oxford University Press, 1961), 30-65.

38. From the anonymous *Wit's Recreation* (London, 1667), sig. L8r. On the basis of an attribution of this poem to Jonson in *The Gentlemen's Magazine,* the editors of *Ben Jonson* included this comic epitaph among the poet's apocrypha (7:444).

39. *The Poems and Fables of John Dryden,* ed. James Kinsley (Oxford: Oxford University Press, 1962), 22-32.

40. Heward, *Matthew Hale,* 109-14; Richard Baxter's *Additional Notes on the Life of Sir M. Hale* and Gilbert Burnet's *The Life and Death of Sir Matthew Hale,* both published in 1681, concentrate principally upon Hale as a moral and religious author. See also Cotton Mather, *Bonifacius: or An Essay upon the Good,* ed. David Levin (Cambridge: Harvard University Press, 1966), 120-31.

41. Theodore F. T. Plucknett, *Concise History of the Common Law,* 5th ed. (Boston: Little Brown, 1956), 245-48, and references.

42. Joseph Addison and Richard Steele, *The Tatler,* ed. G. A. Aitken (London: Ballantyne, Hanson & Co. 1898), 1:122-24.

43. Addison and Steele, *The Spectator,* nos. 38, 467, and see the dedication to vol. 8 of *The Tatler.*

44. For his legal career, see C. H. S. Fifoot, *Lord Mansfield* (Oxford: Oxford University Press, 1936).

45. Fortescue plays a leading role in Alexander Pope's "First Satire of the Second Book of Horace," in *Imitations of Horace,* ed. John Butt (London: Methuen, 1939), 4:1-21. This poem begins with the lines "I come to counsel learned in the law: / You'll give me like a friend, both sage and free / Advice, and (as you use) without a fee."

46. Ibid., 4:151. See Ibid., 4:147-53, 175, and 241 for other passages in praise of Murray.

47. Lloyd, *Poems,* 134; *The Poems of Charles Churchill,* ed. James Laver (Methuen, 1970), 12-13, 233n.; and Churchill's *The Ghost,* in *Poems,* 206-10, lines 1797-1934.

48. *Boswell's Life of Johnson,* ed. G. B. Hill and L. F. Powell (Oxford: Clarendon Press, 1934), 4:178 (entry for March 1783).

49. "On the Burning of Lord Mansfield's Library," *The Poetical Works of William Cowper,* ed. H. S. Milford (London: Oxford University Press, 1907), 306.

50. Roscoe Pound, introduction to *Law in Action: An Anthology of the Law in Literature,* ed. Amicus Curiae (New York: Bonanza Books, 1947), xi. This tale has achieved some popularity in the past two centuries: Edward Wynne, *Eunomus, or, Dialogues Concerning the Law and Constitution of England* (London, 1774), 2:36-39; A. Polson, *Law and Lawyers; or, Sketches and Illustrations of Legal History and Biography* (London, 1840), 2:367-88; Irving Browne, *Law and Lawyers in Literature* (Boston: Soule & Bugbee, 1833), 302-3; and F. H. Newmark, "St. Yvo," *Northern Ireland Legal Quarterly* 9 (Spring 1951):172-76, recently reprinted in F. H. Newmark, *Elegantia Juris,* ed. F. J. McIvor (Belfast: Faculty of Law, Queen's University, 1973).

51. Quoted from William Andrews, ed., *The Lawyer in History, Literature, and Humor* (London: W. Andrews, 1896), 28-29.

52. *Sources and Analogues of Chaucer's Canterbury Tales,* ed. W. F. Bryan and Germaine Dempster (New York: Humanities Press, 1958), 270-71.

53. See, for example, lines 567-82 in *Mundus and Infans* and lines 215-24 in *Hyckescorner,* both plays ca. 1515-1520, in *Specimens of the Pre-Shakespearean Drama,* ed. J. M. Manly (1897, reprint; New York: Dover, 1967), 1:372, 393-94.

54. *Elizabethan History Plays,* ed. W. A. Armstrong (London: Oxford University Press, 1965), 167-260.

55. Thomas Favent, *Historia mirabilis parliamenti,* ed. May McKisack, Camden 3rd ser., vol. 37 (London: Camden Society, 1926), 18. Tresilian was also popularized as the architypically corrupt judge in *The Mirror for Magistrates,* ed. Lily B. Campbell (Cambridge: Cambridge University Press, 1938), 73-80.

56. Fifoot, *History and Sources of the Common Law,* 90-91, 343-44; Baker, *Introduction to English Legal History,* 187.

57. *The Returne of the Knight of the Poste,* sig. C3v.

58. W. D. Macray, *The Pilgrimage to Parnassus, With the Two Parts of the Return from Parnassus* (Oxford: Oxford University Press, 1886), 4.2; and *Club Law,* ed. G. C. Moore-Smith (Cambridge: Cambridge University Press).

59. J. H. Baker, "Solicitors and the Law of Maintenance," *CLJ* 32 (April 1973):56-80.

60. John Day, *Law-Tricks* (Oxford: Malone Society, 1950), 63-64.

61. Middleton, *Works* 1:405-9.

62. Quoted from John Marston's "Cynic Satire," in *Tudor Verse Satire,* ed. K. W. Gransden (London: Athlone Press, 1970), 113.

63. See, for example, Edward Hake, *Epieikeia, A Dialogue on Equity in Three Parts,* ed. D. E. C. Yale (New Haven: Yale University Press, 1953).

64. Edward Hake, *Newes out of Powles Churchyarde,* ed. Charles Edmonds (London, 1872), sigs. B4v, B6v-B7r, Clv.

65. Stubbes, *Anatomy of Abuses* 1:117.

66. Tisdale's *Lawyer's Philosophy,* sigs. C6v-C7r.

67. Earle, *Micro-cosmographie,* 54; Stephens, *Satyrical Essayes,* 281-82; *Overburian Characters,* 31; and Webster, *Complete Works* 4:35.

68. William Cole informs the profession that God has heard of their corruption: "Ye are weighed in the balance of Justice, ye are found as light as chaff; there is a wind risen up, that will blow your interest into the land of oblivion" *A Rod for the Lawyers* (1659) in *Harleian Miscellany* (London: Harleian Society, 1809), 4:326.

69. Gerard Winstanley, "A Watch-Word to the City of London," in his *The Law of Freedom,* ed. Christopher Hill (London: Pelican Classics, 1973), 134-35.

70. Winstanley, "A New-year's Gift for the Parliament and Army," *Law of Freedom,* 201.

71. *Harleian Miscellany* 4:389.

72. *Acts and Ordinances of the Interregnum, 1642-1660,* ed. C. H. Firth and R. S. Rait (London: HMSO, 1911), 2:455-56.

73. Mercurius Rhadamanthus, *The Chiefe Iudge of Hell,* no. 8, 18 July 1653, sig. D1r. The periodical, collected among the Thomason Tracts of the British Library, was offered as a weekly "Inquisition, and Survey of all the Courts in *England,* perfectly discovering all

the Corruptions, Briberies, Extortions, Cruelties, Oppressions, and Knaveries, Exercised by his Brethren the Professors thereof."

74. Ibid. For an interesting assessment of the role of law in the politics of the Commonwealth period, see E. W. Ives, "Social Change and the Law," in his *The English Revolution, 1600-1660* (New York: Harper Torchbooks, 1971), 115-30.

75. See "The Records in English Act," 4 Geo, II, c. 26. A continuing debate in the periodicals indicates that the problem of legal language and record-keeping was a lively issue prior to the passing of the Act. One writer in the *Daily Courant,* 4 March 1731, offers some good reasons against the proposed reform: that the Latin terms were "terms of art," established by centuries of usage, and these could only be abolished at the risk of causing great uncertainty in the law; that a time would come when few will be able to read the ancient records; and that the use of English in Chancery had neither simplified the law nor affected its prolixity. A further criticism reminds the reader that "in *Oliver's* Time an Attempt was made to render Law-Proceedings into *English,* but was attended with so many Inconveniences, that at the Restauration the *Latin* was again restored" (*Gentleman's Magazine* 1:98). See also *Law Quibbles; or A Treatise of the Evasions, Tricks, Turns and Quibbles Commonly Used in the Profession of the Law* (London, 1724), sig. F3v, where the author looks favorably upon the languages of antiquity and states that Law French was not originally design'd to keep People in Ignorance as some Persons imagine, or to make the Study of the Law difficult."

76. *POAS* 1:158.

77. *POAS* 2:351-55. *The Diary of John Milward,* ed. Caroline Robbins (Cambridge: Cambridge University Press, 1938), 166-70, 243, describes the parliamentary inquiry concerning the conduct of Keeling LCJ and Tyrrel J in 1667-1668. A bill against intimidation of juries is here proposed, debated, and given a second reading before passing into law. Like many such enactments, this law failed for lack of any means for enforcement.

78. See *POAS* 2:281-91, for a series of Whig satires attributed to Stephen College. The quoted passage is from "Lampoon on Lord Scroggs," 2:289, lines 12-14. Michael Landon gives a brief account of the trial and execution of College for seditious words in 1681 (*The Triumph of the Lawyers* [University, Ala.: University of Alabama Press, 1970], 103).

79. *Hell's Higher Court of Justice; or, The Triall of the Three Politick Ghosts* (London, 1661), a copy of which is preserved in the British Library.

80. Charles Gildon, *Nuncius Infernalis* (London, 1692), sigs. C2r-D4r.

81. Ward, canto 5, *A Journey to Hell,* sigs. E2v-H1r.

82. *Poor Robins Dream, or Visions of Hell* (London, 1681), sig. A2r.

83. In *Poems, 1649-1727,* a collection of broadside ballads in the British Library (11602.1.12.), printed by R. N., Fleetstreet, 1712.

84. "A True and Faithful Narrative of What Passed in London," *Satires and Personal Writings by Jonathan Swift,* ed. W. A. Eddy (London: Oxford University Press, 1932), 93-94. This tract, which has been variously attributed to Pope, Gay, or Swift, is not included in the Davis edition. See also "Verses on the Death of Dr. Swift," *The Poems of Jonathan Swift,* ed. Harold Williams (Oxford: Clarendon Press, 1937), 2:569-70:

> A wicked Monster on the Bench,
> Whose Fury Blood could never quench

> As vile and profligate a Villain,
> As modern *Scroggs,* or old *Tressilian;*
> Who long all Justice has discarded,
> Nor fear'd he GOD, nor Man regarded;
> Vow'd on the Dean his Rage to vent;
> And make him of his Zeal repent;
> But Heav'n his Innocence defends,
> The grateful People stand his Friends:
> Not strains of Law, nor Judges Frown,
> Nor Topicks brought to please the Crown,
> Nor Witness hir'd, nor Jury pick'd,
> Prevail to bring him in convict (lines 417-30).

These lines are directed at William Whitshed, Lord Chief Justice of Ireland. Elsewhere, Swift laments the abdication of legal responsibility of the English in Ireland and expresses his approval of "the wisdom of the *Antients,* who after Astraea had fled the Earth, at least took Care to provide *three upright Judges in Hell*' (*The Intelligencer,* no. 19, in *The Prose Works,* 12:57). These great three, Aeacus, Minos, and Rhadamanthus, continually appear in the law satire of the eighteenth century.

85. This poem, ascribed to Richard Burridge, is in the British Library collection, 993.e.49. (5.).

86. Defoe, "The True-Born Englishman," in *POAS* 6:267.

87. *Hell in an Uproar,* 14-15.

88. Dim Sasson, *Law Vision: or, Pills for Posterity* (London, 1736).

89. Vision 10, 133-44.

90. Vision 1, 23.

91. Vision 3, 49-52.

92. Vision 1, 28-29; vision 10, 135.

93. This poem is preserved in British Library collection 11630.c.14. (15.).

94. Churchill, *The Ghost,* in *Poems,* 206-10; the full text of *A Fragment of an Epic Poem* is in *The Works of John Hall-Stephenson, Esq.* (London, 1795), 2:147-70. First published as *An Essay upon the King's Friends* (London, 1776), this satire was thought, initially, to be the work of Churchill. The correct authorship has recently been determined by Lodwick Hartley, in "Sterne's Eugenius as Indiscreet Author: The Literary Career of John Hall-Stephenson," *PMLA* 86 (May 1971):439-41.

95. Fielding, *Works* 10:232.

96. Quoted from Robert Collison, *The Story of Street Literature: Forerunner of the Popular Press* (Santa Barbara: ABC-CLIO, 1973), 84.

97. "St. Peter *v.* A Lawyer," in Browne, *Law and Literature,* 303-06. This poem, written around 1800, is a fragment.

98. *Pettifoggers: A Satire in Hudibrastick Verse, Displaying the Various Frauds, Deceits, and Knavish Practices, of the Pettifogging Counsellors, Attornies, Solicitors, and Clerks, etc.* (London, 1723), sig. B3v.

99. Defoe, *A Hymn to the Pillory,* in *POAS* 6:585-605. Lines 25-28 are quoted.

100. *The Lawyers Disbanded: or, The Temple in an Uproar* (London, 1745), a copy of which is preserved in the British Library.

Chapter 5. Satirical Representations: Lovers and Fools

1. Lewis Carroll, "You Are Old, Father William," in *The Oxford Book of Children's Verse,* ed. Iona and Peter Opie (Oxford: Oxford University Press, 1973), 239-40, lines 21-24.

2. Prest, *Inns of Court,* 91-100l and for Justice Shallow, see *2 Henry IV* (3.2.21-24).

3. Barrey, *Ram-Alley,* sig. D4v.

4. Finkelpearl, *Marston of the Middle Temple,* 261-64.

5. *Zepheria* (Manchester: The Spenser Society, 1869). See sonnets 20, 21, 37 for the usage of legal jargon, but 5, 6, 16, 26, 35, 38, 40 also employ legal terms and metaphors.

6. *The Poems of John Donne,* ed. Sir Herbert Grierson (London: Oxford University Press, 1933), 134, lines 45-48.

7. Sir John Davies, *The Complete Poems* 2:59-62.

8. *Overburian Characters,* 31.

9. This passage cited from Browne, *Law and Lawyers,* 51.

10. Browne, *Law and Lawyers,* 42.

11. Tucker, ed., "Parkhurst's Ignoramus" (1.4.48-56C), 1:17; Edward Ravenscroft, *The English Lawyer,* sig. B4r.

12. Ruggle, *Ignoramus,* 59-60.

13. Ibid., 62-63.

14. J. L. Van Gundy, *Ignoramus* (Lancaster, Pa.: New Era Printing, 1906), 71-98.

15. Samuel Butler, *Hudibras,* ed. John Wilders (Oxford: Oxford University Press, 1967), 2.1.737-40.

16. Edward F. J. Tucker, "*Ignoramus* and Seventeenth-Century Satire of the Law," *Harvard Library Bulletin* 19 (July 1971):328-29.

17. Gildon, *Nuncius Infernalis,* sigs. C2r-D4r.

18. Ibid., sig. D3v.

19. Ward, *Journey to Hell,* sigs. E2v-F1r.

20. *POAS* 6:188, lines 433-42. The Clito of this passage is Lovell, and Cowper is pilloried as Casco.

21. *POAS* 6:589. Seditious libel is "written censure upon public men for their conduct as such, or upon the laws, or upon the institutions of our country"; see Sir James F. Stephen, *A History of the Criminal Law of England* (London: Macmillan, 1883), 2:348.

22. See *The Tatler,* 1, no. 84; *The Spectator,* no. 534, 4:407-8; and *The Diary of Dudley Ryder,* 71-72, 85, 138.

23. Swift, "A Project for the Advancement of Religion and the Reformation of Manners," in *The Prose Works* 2:55.

24. "Helter Skelter, or The Hue and Cry after the Attornies, Going to Ride the Circuit," in *The Poems of Jonathan Swift,* ed. Harold Williams (Oxford: Clarendon Press, 1937), 2:572-74.

25. *The Wit's Miscellany* (London, 1774), 134-35.

26. *The Lawyer and Nell; or, The Lawyer Humbugg'd* (Glasgow, 1808), a copy of which is preserved in the British Library.

27. *Mundus et Infans,* in *Specimens of Pre-Shakespearean Drama* 1:372, lines 576-83; *Hyckescorner,* ibid., 1:394, line 222.

28. I have consulted the copy in the Harvard Law Library. Callis refers to Ruggle and his

party as "kinsmen in ignorance." See also the anonymous *An Ignoramus Found upon the Last Article* (1661).

29. The returning of bills ignoramus was a device used by many humanitarian citizens to mitigate the severity of criminal trials and thus to save many offenders from the gallows. See J. S. Cockburn's *A History of English Assizes 1558-1714* (Cambridge: Cambridge University Press, 1972), 127.

30. A copy of this tract is in the Houghton Library collection.

31. Quoted from the broadside ballad in the Houghton Library.

32. Tucker, "Harvard Manuscript of Parkhurst's *Ignoramus*," 7, 17n.

33. Van Gundy, *Ignoramus,* 1-4; George Dyer, *An English Prologue and Epilogue to the Latin Comedy of Ignoramus* (London, 1797), 6, lists six performances between 1712 and 1797. Several editions at the turn of the century suggest further productions of the play before 1712.

34. Richard Hosley, "The Formal Influence of Plautus and Terence," *Elizabethan Theatre,* ed. J. R. Brown and Bernard Harris, Stratford-Upon-Avon Studies, no. 9 (New York: St. Martin's Press, 1967), 131-45.

35. Louise G. Clubb, *Giambattista Della Porta: Dramatist* (Princeton: Princeton University Press, 1965), 284-90; Van Gundy, *Ignoramus,* 61.

36. Elyot, *The Governour,* 51.

37. British Library MS. Royal 18.A.50, fol. 6v.

38. British Library MS. Cotton Faustina C.xi, fols. 11v-12r.

39. For comments on the gradual decay of the legal profession through the admission of lower-class students, see the anonymous *The Institution of a Gentleman* (London, 1568), sig. E3; and Lawrence Humphrey, *The Nobles, or of Nobility* (London, 1563), sig. Q5v. Though the alarm was somewhat exaggerated, these and following citations indicate genuine concern for dilution of standards at the Inns.

40. Abraham Fraunce, *The Lawiers Logike* (London, 1588), sig. Q4r-v.

41. Davies, *Complete Poems* 2:24.

42. Cyril Tourneur, *The Revenger's Tragedy,* ed. Brian Gibbons (London: Benn, 1967), 75-76 (4.2.58-66).

43. Lenton, *Characterismi,* sigs. B4v-F4v; *Overburian Characters,* 30.

44. *Overburian Characters,* 45-46.

45. Earle, *Micro-cosmographie,* 54; Saltonstall, *Picturae Loquentes,* 34.

46. Gransden, *Tudor Verse Satire,* 113; *Characters and Passages from Note-Books,* ed. A. R. Waller (Cambridge: Putnam, 1908). 73; "Parkhurst's Ignoramus," ed. Tucker, Prologue, lines 11-12.

47. This passage is later lifted verbatim by the author of *The Pettifoggers* (London, 1723), sig. A4r. See also *Cheife Iudge of Hell,* no. 4, sigs. D1r-v.

48. I have used the Houghton Library quarto.

49. *Ignoramus,* ed. Hawkins, 47 (1.3).

50. Edward Grimston, *The Lawyer's Fortune; or, Love in a Hollow Tree* (London, 1705).

51. *The Funeral,* in *The Plays of Richard Steele,* ed. Shirley Strum Kenny (Oxford: Oxford University Press, 1971), 20-21.

52. John Arbuthnot, *The History of John Bull,* ed. Herman Teerink (Amsterdam: H. J. Paris, 1925), 141, passim.

53. Ibid., 143.

54. Swift, *Gulliver's Travels,* in *The Prose Works* 11:248-50.

55. It was largely due to Swift's influence that the Irish Commons reacted against the agitation for repeal of the Test Act in 1733. In addition to a number of tracts written by Swift and his supporters, the fiery Dean penned a biting satire against several of his opponents in "On the Words Brother Protestants and Fellow Christians," in which he lampoons Serjeant Richard Bettesworth:

> Thus at the Bar that Booby Bettesworth,
> Tho' Half a Crown o'er-pays his Sweat's Worth;
> Who knows in Law, nor Text, nor Margent,
> Calls *Singleton* his Brother Serjeant.
> (lines 26-29)

This scathing satire (see *Swift's Poems* 3:812), led to a violent confrontation between Swift and Bettesworth, but the lawyer's threats did not deter the dean or his party. He followed the altercation with "An Epigram Inscribed to the Honourable Serjeant Kite" (Ibid., 3:817-18) while anonymous supporters (and perhaps Swift himself) contributed another lampoon entitled "The Yahoo's Overthrow; or, The Kevan Bayl's New Ballad" upon Serjeant Kite and his insulting behavior (Ibid., 3:814-17):

> Now B—th, that booby, and S—l in grain,
> Has insulted us all by insulting the Dean.
> *Knock him down, down, down, knock him down.*
>
> The Dean and his merits we ev'ry one know,
> But this skip of a Lawyer, where the De'el did he grow?
> How greater's his merit at four Courts or House,
> Than the barking of Towzer, or leap of a louse?
> *Knock him down,* &c.
>
> That he came from the Temple, his morals do show,
> But where his deep law is, few mortals yet know:
> His rhet'ric, bombast, silly jests, are by far
> More like to lampooning than pleading at bar.
> *Knock him down,* &c.
> (lines 3-15)

In these and other pieces, Serjeant Richard Bettesworth is characterized as a pettifogging ignoramus of no particular consequence and certainly of no real threat to the dean or to the Tory cause.

56. Louis I. Bredvold, "The Gloom of the Tory Satirists," in *Man versus Society in Eighteenth-Century Britain,* ed. James L. Clifford (Cambridge: Cambridge University Press, 1968), 5.

57. See Jonathan Swift, "Thoughts on Various Subjects," *The Prose Works* 4:246. Swift wonders, "If Books and Laws continue to increase as they have done for fifty years past; I am in some Concern for future Ages, how any Man will be learned, or any Man a Lawyer."

58. *The Diary and Correspondence of John Evelyn,* ed. William Bray (London: G. Bell, 1909), 1:730.

59. *The Pettifoggers,* sig. B1v.

60. See the entry for 27 November 1739 of Henry Fielding's *The Champion,* in *Works* 15:80-81.

61. Edward F. J. Tucker, "Fielding and Rolle's Abridgement," *Modern Philology* 79 (November 1981):173-76, shows the relationship between the Champion's legal opinion and the citations from Rolle's abridgement.

62. Cited from "A Specimen of Scriblerus's Reports," in *The Works of Alexander Pope,* ed. Whitwell Elwin and W. J. Courthope (London: J. Murray, 1886), 10:430-34.

63. Edward Phillips, *The Mock Lawyer* (London, 1733), sigs. C1r-C2r.

64. Fielding, *Works* 15:112-15.

65. See Tobias Smollett's *Sir Launcelot Greaves,* ed. David Evans (Oxford: Oxford University Press, 1973), 14, where the hero styles himself a "coadjutor to the law, and even to remedy evils which the law cannot reach; to detect fraud and treason, abase insolence, mortify pride, discourage slander, disgrace immodesty, and stigmatize ingratitude," This resolution accords well with a sentiment expressed in a letter which Smollett wrote to Alexander Hume Campbell: that one's chief obligation is to consult that "Court of Honour which every man of honour holds in his own breast" (*The Letters of Tobias Smollett,* ed. Lewis M. Knapp [Oxford: Oxford University Press, 1970], 22).

66. In Gay's fables, the lawyer is usually portrayed as a fox, but his most extensive attack upon abuses of the law is his *Beggar's Opera* (1728). "Lectures on Heads" (1762) in *The Works of George Stevens* (London, 1807), 31-33, 40-42, furnishes lampoons of legal language and conduct.

67. *Works of George Stevens,* 31.

68. Jones, *Henry Fielding, Novelist and Magistrate,* 84-86, 118-19, 132-33.

69. Smollett, *Sir Launcelot Greaves,* 2.

Epilogue

1. For extensive analysis of the influence of reform movements upon literature, see Patrick Brantlinger, *The Spirit of Reform: British Literature and Politics, 1832-1867* (Cambridge: Harvard University Press). Other useful studies of law and literature in the later period include Philip Collins's *Dickens and Crime,* Cambridge Studies in Criminology vols. 17 (London: Macmillan, 1965); Henry S. Drinker, *The Lawyers of Anthony Trollope* (New York: The Grolier Club, 1950); and Coral Lansbury, *The Reasonable Man: Trollope's Legal Fiction* (Princeton: Princeton University Press, 1981).

2. Ronald Paulson, *Satire and Novel in Eighteenth-Century England* (New Haven: Yale University Press, 1967), 108, suggests that the satiric impulse in Fielding's major novels is still present but subordinated to the articulation of moral and social norms. I agree with this general assessment since extensive treatment of social problems requires deeper character analysis than the satiric representations of earlier comedy will afford. See Ian Watt, *The Rise of the Novel* (Berkeley: University of California Press, 1959), 19-20, on Fielding's use of type-names.

Index